"Twenty-five years ago I watched the Lewis family work through the brokenness, pain and loss described in *Bittersweet*. Now, twenty-five years later, I am also witnessing the remarkable restoration and joy that God has brought to the whole family. You will be encouraged that God does not forget the cries of our heart."

Lee Bennett
Senior Pastor
Northwest Community Church, Bothell, Washington

"*Bittersweet* is pure joy. Bring handkerchiefs! Gay Lewis frames a window to God's heart in her deeply moving story of her daughter's unplanned pregnancy. She walks us through the gripping pain of crisis in a tightly knit family, the bittersweet loss of her first granddaughter given for adoption, and the restoration of her own daughter. Over the years the family walks paths of renewal and grace they never expected to encounter. Then, in a finish that only God could fashion, we are shown that He is always at work, even when we can't see Him, preparing the best for us."

Austin Boyd
Navy pilot, astronaut candidate finalist,
Inventive engineer (www.austinboyd.com),
Award-winning novelist, Mars Hill Classified Trilogy
Speaker and fund-raiser for crisis pregnancy ministries
Brownsboro, Alabama

"There are so many tragic and unhappy stories about unexpected and unwanted pregnancies out of wedlock. Gay Lewis poignantly shares one that is beautifully framed in the context of the grace and transforming love of Jesus Christ. This story is born out of her family's personal pain and heartache, and majestically moves into joy and celebration by the touch of the Master's hand."

Doug Burleigh
Past President of Young Life
Associate, International Foundation,
Washington, D.C.

BITTERSWEET

BITTERSWEET
The Restoration Continues

Gay Lewis

WINEPRESS WP PUBLISHING

WinePress Publishing (PO Box 428, Enumclaw, WA 98022) functions only as book publisher. As such, the ultimate design, content, editorial accuracy, and views expressed or implied in this work are those of the author.

Unless otherwise noted, all Scriptures are taken from the *Holy Bible, New International Version®, NIV®*.Copyright © 1973, 1978, 1984 by the International Bible Society. Used by permission of Zondervan. All rights reserved.

Scripture references marked KJV are taken from the *King James Version* of the Bible.

Scripture references marked RSV are taken from the *Revised Standard Version* of the Bible, copyright 1952 [2nd edition, 1971] by the Division of Christian Education of the National Council of the Churches of Christ in the United States of America. Used by permission. All rights reserved.

ISBN 13: 978-1-57921-944-4
ISBN 10: 1-57921-944-6
Library of Congress Catalog Card Number: 2007942000

CONTENTS

FOREWORD

Beauty for ashes, the oil of joy for mourning, the
garment of praise for the spirit of heaviness . . .

—Isaiah 61:3 KJV

As I read through this book, written by my mother, I realize
how much of my personal life I'm sharing. It scares me. Part of
me wants to withdraw, burying the experience of the past.

But stronger than my fear is my desire to reach out to other hurting
women, men, and children—especially the many who are affected in
some way by an unwanted pregnancy.

Your situation may be similar to mine or completely different. The
struggle each one of us experiences is unique. To compare circumstances is not the purpose of this book. I simply want you to see that
God can be trusted. There *is* healing, and every part of our lives can
be transformed into something beautiful.

Though I have never walked in your shoes, I know about the ashes,
the mourning, and the heaviness. But I also know that there is hope!
And beauty! And, yes, even joy!

Our God will see you through your crisis. He doesn't close His eyes and wait until it's over. Because of this aspect of His character we can walk through anything in forgiveness, confidence, and peace.

—Laurie Lewis Carr

Part One

BITTERSWEET

. . . The Restoration Continues . . .

1
"I KNOW I'M PREGNANT"

I felt sick inside." Laurie's voice was tight with remembered pain. "Sick and cold. At the same time it was like I couldn't feel anything at all. I remember there was an upside-down water jug in the health clinic waiting room. It was all sweaty and green and cold-looking, just like the walls in the room. There were rows of connected plastic chairs, back to back, and little white pamphlets and folders on tables and in racks."

Laurie suddenly looked at me.

"Mom, I knew that test would be just a formality. I'd been so tired and sore and I always had a crampy feeling. Besides, my period was three weeks late."

I ached for my daughter. What a thing to have to go through anywhere, let alone a thousand miles from home. She was in Bible school, three and a half weeks into her first quarter, when she had made that appointment.

"Did you go to the clinic alone?" I asked.

Laurie sighed. "No. I'd told Collette and Tracy I thought I was pregnant. I hadn't known them for very long, but I guess I felt safe telling them. Anyway, they sat with me while I waited to go in."

1

She lifted her head with a pleading look in her eyes. "It's really hard to talk about this. I might cry."

"You don't have to tell me about it if you don't want to," I assured her.

"But I do want to. I need to. I guess I've buried the whole experience because it was too painful to think about. It's time to get it out."

Laurie was usually bright and energetic. Her tall, slim figure and blonde hair attracted attention wherever she went. She was warm and caring, and she had a glowing, infectious smile. It hurt to see her so sad and wan.

She stared out the window again. "Sitting there in the clinic, I felt like I wasn't really there. Collette and Tracy were laughing and talking, and I tried to join in. But it was like I was watching some other girl in a movie instead of me. I could hear that other girl's thoughts loud and clear, while her friends talked in the background.

"There were a dozen or so girls in the waiting room with us, and they had also come in for pregnancy tests. They were all nicely dressed, probably from normal, middle-class families. They looked just like me." Her eyes brimmed with tears. "But I felt in the lowest of classes, just because I was there. I thought about the summer before—the way I was then. That 'me' seemed like somebody I used to know, not the person sitting there in that cold, green room."

The tears spilled over and she had to stop for a few minutes. I sat and waited, trying not to cry myself.

Laurie sighed and took up her story. "Somebody brought me forms to fill out. That gave me something to think about for a few minutes. When the nurse called my name, I followed her into the office.

"Several older ladies worked there. I thought, *They're probably all moms.* They looked at me as I walked by, and their eyes seemed to say, 'Well, here comes another one.'

"The nurse handed me a little plastic cup and took me to a small restroom to leave a urine sample. Then I went back to the waiting room until they called me with the test results. Collette and Tracy were talking about something funny that happened at school. I tried to listen to them, but I kept thinking, *I know I'm pregnant. What am I going to do? What is Rick[1] going to say? How can I put my family through this?* I had to blink back the tears."

I took a drink of my now cool tea. I knew exactly what she meant. "When did you start thinking something might be wrong?" I asked.

"During my first week at school I started to worry. I knew that Rick and I had gotten much too involved during the summer. When I was pretty certain I was pregnant, I began to think about abortion. Wouldn't it be OK so early in a pregnancy? It wasn't actually a person yet, was it?

"But also in that first week of school, we were given copies of a regular prayer-newsletter. One of the main articles that month told the facts of abortion, and I had to think twice. Then God started speaking to me about the tiny, innocent lives that get thrown away so easily every day. I underlined Psalm 139:13–16 in my Bible."

I reached for my husband's Bible lying on the table and turned to those verses. "For you created my inmost being; you knit me together in my mother's womb. I praise you because I am fearfully and wonderfully made; your works are wonderful, I know that full well. My frame was not hidden from you when I was made in the secret place. When I was woven together in the depths of the earth, your eyes saw my unformed body. All the days ordained for me were written in your book before one of them came to be."

Laurie nodded her head. "I saw that if I were pregnant, then God already knew my baby and loved it as a tiny human being. How could I do any less?"

As Laurie reached for the teapot and refilled our cups, I quietly thanked God that He had faithfully led her into that firm decision.

She took a sip. "OK, so there I was, still sitting in that awful room. I looked again at the other girls who were waiting. They had each had their turn in the office just as I had. I wondered if they all felt as numb and sick as I did.

"Every once in a while a nurse would come out and talk quietly to one of the girls. Then the girl would get up and leave. But others were called back into the office.

---

[1] Rick was fictionally called "Mark" in the original *Bittersweet*.

"The nurse came out and said, 'Laurie Lewis?' and motioned me to come with her. I felt dizzy, like it must be some other person who was standing up and walking toward her.

"Then the nurse said, 'Oh, I'm sorry! I said the wrong name!' And she called someone else.

"I sat down again and waited for my heart to stop racing. Tracy and Collette kept telling me not to worry. 'Every year girls come to the school thinking they're pregnant and they never are.' Their words still sounded like background conversation.

"Then my name was called for real, and I felt like I was dreaming. I followed the nurse into a little room. Everything seemed so small. The room, the window, the desk. And it all got smaller when she closed the door.

"A social worker sat behind the little desk. She pointed to an empty chair and I sat.

"'Your test was positive.'

"That's all she said. I got tingly and hot. I thought I might throw up. The only answer I could get out was, 'Uh-huh.'

"The lady asked, 'How do you feel about that?'

"Then I started to cry. The woman smiled and said, 'That's what I thought.' She handed me some tissues. Then she asked questions about my family, about Rick, and about my plans for the future.

"'I don't intend to marry Rick.'

"She nodded. 'Have you considered abortion?'

"'No, I definitely don't want an abortion.'

"But the woman was persistent. She went on. 'OK, but let me just tell you a little bit about it. It's no big thing, you know. It's certainly no big surgery, just a simple visit to the doctor's office. In and out and it's all over with. Would you like a list of the doctors who perform abortions here in the city?' She reached for a desk drawer.

"'No!' I cried. 'I don't want to have it or even see it!'

"The woman was very kind. She was obviously trying to give me what she thought was the easiest way out. She asked more questions, and I told her I wasn't sure what I would do. 'But I'm considering adoption.'

"The woman looked surprised. 'Why would you do that? Abortion is so much simpler.'

"Several more times she asked me, 'Are you sure you don't want that list?' I just kept saying no. When I stood up to go, she said, 'Do call me and let me know what you decide.'

"I was in a daze when I walked back into the waiting room. For a second or two I stood staring at Collette and Tracy as if I didn't even see them. Then something snapped inside of me. I turned and ran for an exit door."

Laurie's cheeks were flushed and her eyes full of intense emotion, but she kept on talking. "I pushed through the door, and a strange, sobbing sound came from my throat. The door hit a metal garbage can outside. The crash seemed so loud. I ran down a ramp and into the parking lot. I stopped, not knowing what I wanted to do or where I wanted to go. Tracy and Collette caught up with me.

"I managed to say, 'I told you!' They led me to a lawn where we sat down under some trees. I was crying harder by then, and they were wonderfully kind. When I finally stopped crying enough to talk, I told them what had happened.

"Collette said, 'But, Laurie, those health clinic tests aren't always accurate. If you really want to be sure, then let's go to the hospital and get a blood test.'

"I let them drive me to the hospital, and sat in the car while they went in. While I waited, the sun on my arm and shoulder made me hot, and I rolled down the car window. I had forgotten that it was a beautiful, sunny day. There was a cool breeze blowing.

"The girls came back before very long. Tracy said, 'We asked where to have a pregnancy test. We told them where you had gotten the other one. They called the clinic, and that lady wants to see you again.'

"So we drove back and the woman came outside to see me. She looked like she thought we had been complaining about her. She asked me if I had a question.

"I said, 'No, but my friends wanted to be sure that the test was right.'

"Then the woman turned to Collette and Tracy. 'It's natural to want to protect your friend, but you must accept the fact that she is pregnant.'

"We were all pretty quiet when we drove away. We went to a park and talked some more. I told Collette and Tracy that, somehow, I wanted the very best to come out of this. I knew God would take care of me, and maybe He could help me to help other girls."

Laurie grinned wryly at me. "It was pretty hard to believe all that right then," she admitted. "But it helped to say it!"

On one hand my heart broke as I listened to Laurie's story, but on the other I was awed. "Oh, Laurie, I'm so sorry you had to go through all this alone. How long was it before you called us?"

"Well, the night before the test I called Lynn to tell her what was going on. You don't mind that I called her first, do you?"

Lynn was our twenty-year-old daughter. She and Laurie were very close, and they missed each other a lot when Laurie left for school. "Of course I don't mind. I'm just glad you had some family praying for you and loving on you."

Laurie smiled. "I called her back that night. She cried when I told her and said she would do anything she could to help me. I had already told Rick over the phone what I suspected, so I asked her to please call him for me, and tell him that if he was at all concerned about the situation he should call.

"When I told him my fear, he had just said, 'Oh, Laurie, don't worry. You're not pregnant.' He was real confident."

"Wishful thinking," I said.

Laurie nodded. "I'd just told him 'OK, you wait and see,' and I hadn't talked to him since.

"After Lynn called him, he called me. It was, 'Hi, how are you doing?' like nothing was wrong. Then I said, 'I had a pregnancy test today. It was positive.' Silence. And then, so quietly I could barely hear him, 'Are you sure?'

"'I'm sure, and I'm going to have the baby.'

"He absolutely couldn't accept that. He thought abortion was the only acceptable, sensible solution. 'You're going to wreck your life! You can't do it. I won't let you. This is one time I'm going to put my foot down! And I'm not going to change my mind.' He sounded desperate.

"'Stop, Rick. I'm here at this school because I want to make a commitment to Jesus. I've already made one bad decision. I can't do

it again. I have to go all the way with Jesus or else go the other direction. I believe abortion is wrong. If I have one, I'll be compromising
what I believe. And I'd have to live with it for the rest of my life.'

"Rick tried to change my mind for a while longer. Then he was
quiet. He laughed softly and said, 'I'm sorry. Whatever you decide,
I'll support you in that. You're a strong person and I admire you
for not just taking the easy way out.' We talked for a while longer
and just before we hung up he said, 'Wouldn't it be weird if we got
married?'

"I didn't say anything right then, but in my heart I knew that our
lives were heading in opposite directions."

Too bad she hadn't thought this way during the summer, but then
we never do plan these things, do we?

"I was sad when we said good-bye," Laurie continued. "I knew
things had changed between us even if he didn't. The love that had
seemed so real was now distant and awkward."

I was relieved at her mature evaluation of their relationship. I
would never want her to marry because she felt she "had to."

"The day after the test began with a sense of unreality. I looked the
same and I felt pretty much the same, but everything was changed. I
knew that my whole life was permanently altered.

"Finally, I knew I had to call you and Dad. I asked my roommates
not to disturb me for a while, and I dragged the telephone into the
bedroom. I sat on the bed with the phone in my lap and dialed your
number. I squeezed my eyes shut, tight. The call went through much
too fast. The minute I heard your voice I started to cry."

2
WHY LAURIE?

When the phone rang that day, I was playing with our two-year-old, Carina. I was laughing as I picked up the receiver. "Hello?"

"Hi, Mom."

"Laurie!" I was delighted to hear her voice.

The extension phone I answered was in the bedroom Laurie had shared with her sixteen-year-old sister, Dawn. At the moment, Dawn was draped across her bed, intently poring over the last *Campus Life* magazine. I settled down on the spare bed to savor every moment of the phone call.

"How are you doing by now?" I asked, leaning back against a pile of colorful pillows. Warm sun streamed through the window. "All settled in?"

"Oh, I'm OK." Laurie sounded strained. In fact, I could barely hear her.

"Is Dad home?"

My stomach tightened, and I suddenly felt cold. Something was wrong. "No. Why?"

There was a long silence before she answered.

"Oh, Mom! I don't want to do this to you!" Laurie was sobbing and could hardly speak. "I'm pregnant."

My ears started buzzing and my eyes blurred as I tried to take in what she had said. It seemed as if the sun disappeared, and a heavy, dark cloud settled down around me and the phone. I held on to the receiver with both hands, trying to keep control of myself. After all, hadn't I always rehearsed our reaction if this should ever happen to one of our daughters? I'd be calm and cool, and I'd assure her that our love for her wasn't threatened in any way. Then I'd help her begin to work through the long months ahead.

But now, all I wanted to do was cry. I wasn't angry at Laurie, but I was angry. Anger was the only available emotion to camouflage the intense pain. I wanted to throw the telephone through the window. How could that small, cold instrument bring such devastating news?

There was so much chaos inside me that I couldn't respond in the way I'd always been sure I would in this situation. Where were the loving, calm, reassuring words I'd been able to speak to other people's daughters? I wanted to run from the duty of this conversation. Go back and play with Carina and pretend it had been a wrong number. Laurie wasn't the sobbing girl on the phone. She was just fine. She was our lovely daughter who was in Bible school.

Our conversation wasn't long. I couldn't think of anything to say. Our basic communication was, "I'm sorry," and, "I love you."

"Mom, please don't tell anybody outside our family. I'm not ready for that yet."

I promised, said good-bye, and hung up the phone. I sat and watched Dawn, still engrossed in her reading.

She doesn't know yet, I thought. She was a busy, purposeful girl, wrapped up in school and sports. Sure, life had its ups and downs, but it was pretty much OK for Dawn.

She chuckled at something she was reading. Her even, white teeth showed in a grin. Short, dark hair curled neatly around her face in a style that wouldn't misbehave even at a track meet.

"Dawn." I didn't want to tell her, but I found myself walking toward her bed.

"Yes?" She tore her eyes from her magazine.

"That was Laurie."

Dawn's clear, gray-blue eyes lit up. "It was?" Then she frowned. "Why didn't you let me talk to her? I didn't get to last time either."

"Dawn, Laurie's pregnant," I blurted.

She looked as if I'd slapped her. "She's what?" She was on her feet now. Tears filled her eyes. "Mom!" She came toward me. "Oh, Mom!"

We held each other and cried for a while. It felt good to cry. The anger and pain seemed to flow out with the tears. We both sat down rather weakly on a bed.

Suddenly I realized that Carina had been out of sight for some time. It's not a good idea for a two-year-old to be out of sight, and I didn't remember seeing her since about halfway through my conversation with Laurie.

"Carina!" I called.

"Mommy! Okay!" she answered from the kitchen. She shuffled down the hall and into the bedroom clutching a big pile of strange-looking little parcels to her chest. Beaming at me, my resourceful daughter deposited about fifty crumpled-up tea bags in my lap. It was wonderful to laugh, and Carina joined right in. Her blue eyes danced, and the sun shone on her blonde baby curls. Watching her innocent amusement, I felt a sudden stab of pain at the thought of her having to grow up someday.

I went through the necessary motions for the rest of that day. At least there was plenty to keep me busy. We were in the process of moving out of the house. Tom (my husband), Dawn, Carina, and I were going to live temporarily in our thirty-five-foot-long, beautifully remodeled school bus turned motor home. The plan was that we would build a new house soon.

I sorted through belongings, deciding what to store and what to put into the bus, but my mind was moving many times faster than my hands.

"Why, Lord?" Anger rose again in me. "Why now, when Laurie finally is in a place where she could have been free of some of the distractions of life for a while? Lord, You knew the timing of all this. Why didn't You keep it from happening?"

Tears blurred my eyes, and I had to stop taking dishes from the cupboard long enough to reach for a paper towel. I dabbed my eyes dry and went back to work.

I lifted heavy handmade pottery plates off the shelf one at a time, and packed them away between newspapers. No room for those in a bus. Funny. It seemed so irrelevant to be packing dishes at a time like this.

If only I hadn't had to hear this news over the phone! No wonder I couldn't communicate the way I longed to. What was it the experts said: Only 7 percent of interpersonal communication is the spoken word. The other 93 percent is accomplished through body language, tone of voice, and inflection. I'd been so busy trying to keep control that I wondered what my tone of voice and inflection had communicated. Now I just wanted to be with Laurie, hold her, cry with her. I knew I needed to write her a letter. And soon.

Big soup bowls joined the plates in the wooden crate. I didn't hear Dawn walk up behind me.

"Mom?"

I turned to look at her. She was somehow older than she had been that morning.

"Mom, why Laurie?" That's all she said, but I knew exactly what she meant. I'd been asking the same question. Of all our daughters, Laurie had suffered the most trauma in her life. Obviously, she had to take the responsibility for getting herself into this one. But still, it didn't seem fair.

"I feel like somebody died," Dawn whispered.

Again, she expressed my own feelings. "Not exactly like somebody really died," I thought out loud, "but like I *feel* when someone dies."

Dawn nodded, hung her head, and went back to her room.

The shrill ring of the phone beside me made me jump.

"Ring-ring!" Carina hollered, making a dash for it. I let her go ahead and answer it.

"Hi!" she sang into the receiver. "Yah Carina . . . Lynnie!" she said to me.

"OK. Say, 'Here's Mommy.'"

She did, then happily handed over the phone with a big smile.

"Hi, Lynnie." Lynn lived with her aunt, closer to her job. She had called from work.

"Mom—" She hesitated. "Has Laurie called?"

"Yes." The tears came again.

"I'm so glad." Lynn sighed loudly. "She called me last night, and I've been a wreck ever since. I wanted to tell you, but—well, I'm just glad you know."

I heard her blowing her nose. "Mom, I can't understand. Why does it have to be Laurie? She has already had so much pain in her life. Why her?"

Lynn was obviously crying now. I could imagine her wiping furtively at her gray-green eyes, trying to keep her co-workers from seeing her cry. She was soft inside and sometimes it was hard for her to maintain her elegant bearing. She controlled herself, probably shook her curly blonde hair, and sat up straighter.

"I wish I could help her. I'd do anything," she said. "Meantime, the best thing we can do for her is not tell anybody, right?"

"That's what she wants for now," I agreed. "Lynn, keeping quiet won't be easy. We're all hurting, and it's hard to keep it inside. Just call anytime you need to talk."

"Does Dad know yet?"

"No," I groaned. I dreaded having to tell him. He loved his girls so much and was so proud of them.

After my conversation with Lynn, I thought a lot about Tom, working hard at his carpentry job. He'd had open-heart surgery less than a year earlier. God had been good, and his recovery was remarkable, but I hated to see him under pressure.

I knew Tom would handle this news in a totally loving way, but I also knew he would take much of the blame, even more than I. And I wasn't doing too well myself.

"What could I have done to prevent this?" I asked myself over and over.

I knew all about my own human nature and past failures, as well as my current shortcomings.

"What did you expect?" came the accusing voices in my mind. "You just don't measure up as a parent. Now Laurie is going to have to suffer for your flaws and failings. This is your fault."

How could I ever bear that kind of responsibility, especially when human lives were involved—not just Laurie's and ours and the lives of those around us, but a brand-new, innocent life, too. . . .

The answer to my question was simple. I couldn't.

"I am what I am," I told God. "I know I am sinful and unreliable. But I also know that I am forgiven and that You choose not to remember my sin. Somehow teach me to embrace Your forgiveness and see myself as You see me. Somehow let good come out of Laurie's pregnancy."

This would become my constant prayer, though it would take some time to begin to believe the words I spoke. The accusing voices would return to haunt me every time I was discouraged or weak.

Tom and I had spent ten intensive years very much involved with teenagers and young adults. We'd seen every imaginable problem. Over and over we had watched Him turn the worst possible circumstances into examples of His love and forgiveness.

It was just more difficult to believe when it was my own daughter instead of someone else's.

"Dad's here," Dawn announced, hurrying into the kitchen.

I'd been so lost in thought that I wasn't really prepared to face Tom.

Maybe I should have him call Laurie and let her tell him, I thought desperately.

Dawn stood beside me as Tom came in carrying his old, gray lunchbox. He was dusty, which meant he must have been working near plasterboard installation. His blonde curls looked more gray than usual, and the lines beginning to show up in his face appeared a little deeper. He looked tired. Then he saw us standing there, and his blue eyes lit up. "Hi, ladies!"

"Daddy home! Daddy home!" Carina came flying and tackled his long legs. He scooped her up and hugged her, handing me his lunch box. Carina patted his beard and wiggled in his arms until he set her back on the floor.

"How was your day?" he asked, giving me a kiss and a hug. Then he hugged Dawn. She shot a pleading look over his shoulder at me.

"Tom, we have something to tell you," I said.

"Yeah? What?" he asked, releasing Dawn.

I felt sick inside, knowing what I was about to do to him. "Laurie called today."

"She did?" He grinned. "How is she?"

"Tom." I moved toward him. "She just found out that she's pregnant."

The only other times I'd seen that look in his eyes were when someone close to him had died.

"Oh, no," he whispered. I think I cried—again.

We had a quiet dinner that night. All of us were thankful for Carina's noisy diversions, and she was more than delighted to have our undivided attention.

Afterward I stood at the sink rinsing plates. Tom picked up the phone behind me and began to dial. Seven times, then three more. Long distance. He was calling Laurie.

Without even thinking, I dried my hands and headed for our bedroom. As I closed the door I heard Tom say, "Hello? May I speak to Laurie, please?"

Opening the window, I put my head out and stood staring at the toys Carina had left on the deck. Suddenly I felt foolish. What on earth was I doing? Running away? From what? My own daughter?

My eyes filled with tears as I saw that it was pain I was hiding from. I didn't even want to hear Tom's end of the conversation. I didn't want to imagine what Laurie was saying, how she was crying.

With my head out the window, a wall and door between me and the pain, I discovered that it had followed me. It was there with me. In me. With horror I realized that if I continued to run, pain would be my constant foe in the months to come.

I sank onto the bed. "God," I wept, "I don't want to run, except to You. Teach me to face the pain and embrace it. Let it become a friend to help me grow, not an enemy."

Later that night we lay in bed with the light on. Tom's hands were under his head. He stared at the ceiling.

"You know, Gay," he began, "I always said that if this ever happened to one of our girls I'd resign from everything."

"Because you feel responsible?" I asked.

"Yes, partly. My poor little girl. I wish I'd been more available to her last summer," he said painfully.

There didn't seem to be a lot more to say. I didn't know it then, but Tom's visible response was only the tip of the iceberg. Both he and I were to find out the depth of his reaction in the coming days.

3
"BE GENTLE, LORD . . ."

The following weeks brought us all much soul searching. Sure, I knew a million teenagers become pregnant in the United States every year, but just knowing cold statistics didn't help any. They were too remote. But now my own daughter was a statistic.

One million and one.

And Laurie certainly didn't want to be pregnant and unmarried at seventeen.

I knew she was responsible for her own actions, but it seemed to me that there was more at work here than just the sinful nature we all inherited from Adam. I continually asked, "Why?" I searched back further and further into her growing-up years, probing, exploring, trying to unearth experiences or situations that might have contributed somehow to the predicament she now found herself in.

Laurie had been our middle child (before Carina made her appearance!). As any psychologist will tell you, a middle child has his or her own set of problems. But so does the oldest. And the youngest. Certainly birth order is neither an excuse nor an explanation.

Laurie had always been very loving and seemed to need more physical contact than her sisters. It was delightfully easy to give her the extra hugs and kisses, and rock her every night before she went to bed.

Then, when Lynn was ten, Laurie eight, and Dawn six, I lost my mom and best friend after her long battle with cancer. My youngest sister, Tia, also age ten, was devastated. Our dad had been in denial about Mom's health, and Tia had been told she was "getting better."

It had been Mom's desire as well as ours, and was perfectly natural for Tia to move in with us and become a part of our family. It was not a new thing for her to be in our home. Mom and Dad had lived nearby and Tia frequently spent nights and lots of other hours with the girls. They were already like sisters.

All four of the girls attended the private school where Tom taught, and he doubled as their bus driver. The bus sat parked in our driveway when it wasn't being used. Tia, Lynn, Laurie, and Dawn all adjusted well to school and didn't have any obvious problems.

Meanwhile, our family was catapulted into a whirlwind of activity. God began sending young people our way, kids who needed a "place to be," a family to be a part of for a while. We acquired a large extended family in the next nine years or so. Eighty some of them actually lived with us for periods of time, anywhere from two months to two years. A few were legal foster children, and the rest had their parents' permission. Hundreds of others found their way to our door and to our hearts.

The four girls inherited many older brothers and sisters who showered them with all kinds of special privileges and attention. The girls got to see, firsthand, numerous answers to prayer as God changed lives and provided for us in amazing ways. It was a miracle that Tom's teacher's salary alone carried us through those years.

Looking back, it doesn't appear that we neglected our girls. Still, I know it's possible we weren't as sensitive to their needs as we should have been, and in the context of Laurie's situation, I grew uneasy as I remembered that period of time.

Also, during those busy years, because the girls were in a Christian school, we didn't give too much thought to their relationships with their teachers. That was a big mistake, especially for Laurie.

While Laurie was in elementary school, she had a teacher we'll call Mrs. Yeager. She was young, attractive, talented, and very self-confident. She never seemed to run out of ideas or energy. The parents thought she was wonderful. And she was, but we didn't find out until much too late the effect she'd had on our middle daughter.

Laurie hardly ever complained. She had been taught to respect authority, and the years she'd already spent in the school had built well-deserved trust in her teachers. So she naturally assumed that any problem she had at school was her fault.

My heart aches when I think of the pain Laurie quietly endured. Mrs. Yeager was very grade-oriented and quite strict. She tried to help individuals whose grades weren't quite up to her standards by singling them out and putting them on the spot in hopes that they'd shape up.

Laurie was one of those who received special attention. She became terribly fearful of her teacher. When called upon to stand and answer a question, her mind would go blank. Mrs. Yeager would tell her that she should know the answer, so why didn't she? Red faced and stammering, Laurie died a little more each time this humiliation happened. She became convinced she was utterly stupid. When there was something she really didn't understand, she was afraid to ask for help.

One awful day when Laurie couldn't answer a history question, Mrs. Yeager made her sit out in the hall and read her history book. Embarrassed to tears, Laurie tried to make herself as small as possible on the hall floor. But humiliation turned to despair when her dad walked by and saw her sitting there.

"What are you doing out here?" Tom scowled playfully.

Laurie managed a grin, and Tom walked on with a chuckle. During all of this time Laurie's grades remained good. There was never anything to alarm us or to question her about. But Mrs. Yeager apparently thought she could do better and was correct in that assumption. Laurie could have done better if she hadn't been so fearful and paralyzed.

Then there was the black day when Laurie got spanked in front of the whole class. The fact that a number of other students received the same punishment didn't help much. Laurie honestly felt that she hadn't done anything wrong. The only thing worse than humiliation is undeserved humiliation.

Laurie was a good reader, but whenever her turn came to stand beside Mrs. Yeager's desk and read aloud to her, she froze. Her face got red and the words came haltingly, painfully. More and more she became unwilling to try anything new. She hated sports and competition, and was deathly afraid of being in the public eye. It didn't help her damaged self-image when we discovered that she was quite nearsighted, and she had to start wearing glasses. She loathed them and ditched them at every opportunity.

Obviously, personality has much to do with a child's response to a teacher. Lynn had Mrs. Yeager, too, but she easily got straight A's. Lynn was, by nature, more objective and resilient than Laurie, and she didn't seem to be bothered by her time with Mrs. Yeager. We've never heard whether children from other families reacted the way Laurie did.

It is still very painful remembering that part of Laurie's life. If only we had been more observant, more aware. True, Laurie was very quiet about what happened at school. She was afraid we would find out what a "bad girl" she was, so all of our questions were answered positively. School was wonderful, and everything was going fine.

The year after Mrs. Yeager, Laurie had a sensitive teacher. The pressure let up and gradually she began to share with us some of the things that had hurt her so much.

There was only one problem in her new class. The teacher was a writer, and she put great emphasis on this skill. Laurie was already convinced she had no talent in this area. One of the teacher's favorite things was to write the beginning of a story and ask the students to finish it. Everyone else seemed to be able to do something with it, and most of them wrote wonderfully strange and imaginative endings.

Laurie picked up her pencil and went blank. Many times we prodded her imagination and helped her put something together, but she was terribly frustrated each time she tried to write.

"I can't do it!" she wailed.

In sixth grade Laurie had her first experience with the opposite sex. She had much too little confidence to talk to boys. One day a boy named Jim sauntered up.

"Hey, Laurie! Kenny wants me to ask you if you'll go with him." Jim grinned.

"Oh, ah, sure!" Laurie answered, too surprised to even wonder what it all meant. She never did talk to Kenny beyond a red-faced "hi" now and then.

He sent her gifts through Jim, sometimes a quarter, once as much as a whole dollar, and then a big pink ring. Laurie was embarrassed about the whole thing but quite flattered. Finally, though, the fact that she couldn't even find the courage to talk to Kenny bothered her so much that she decided she had to break up with him.

That night she lay in bed and cried, because she didn't want to hurt Kenny's feelings. The next day she sent a girlfriend of hers to tell Kenny the bad news.

Jim was often mean to her after that. "You only liked him for his money!" he accused her.

Laurie's terrible feelings of inferiority colored everything she attempted to do. Sometime in sixth grade she and Lynn began taking piano lessons together. Both girls were very gifted musically, but, even before the first lesson, Laurie was convinced she couldn't learn how to play. She was so upset after that first lesson that we let Lynn continue without her.

In the seventh grade, people began to tell Laurie how pretty she was.

"You're the prettiest girl in the class!" they'd say. "You're so nice!" or "You're sweet!"

And I'm really a nobody inside, Laurie thought. *I never say anything, so all people know is what I look like. Maybe that's all there is to me.*

Again Laurie never said anything about the thoughts she was having. Outwardly, especially at home, she was a happy, energetic child.

Laurie and Kristin had been good friends since kindergarten. During seventh grade the two girls began to spend a lot more time together.

Laurie had always admired Kristin. The talkative, vivacious girl was everything Laurie wanted to be. Kristin always had lots of attention and lots of friends. She had nice things, too—a lovely home, expensive clothes, money. Laurie was never consciously jealous of her, but she often wished she could trade places with her.

When Laurie and Kristin were alone at Kristin's house or ours, the two girls had a wonderful time. Laurie's true personality would emerge, and her wry, boisterous sense of humor kept Kristin in stitches. Laurie traveled and vacationed with Kristin and her family, and Kristin went on outings with us.

She actually convinced Laurie to run track with her, and Laurie discovered she was a good, fast runner. The basketball coach tried to talk her into playing on the team. She was too fearful to try it even though she was extremely fond of the coach.

Talented and very kind, he sensed some of Laurie's lack of confidence and invited her to be team manager so she would feel important. She earned a letter that year and went everywhere with the team. She had a prized picture of the tall, smiling coach and her blonde, happy self, arm and arm in the gym.

Laurie and Kristin, inseparable through junior high, continued to relate wonderfully when they were alone together, and grew to love each other deeply. But the minute other people were around, Laurie became the quiet little mouse that hid in Kristin's shadow.

The boys Laurie's age pretty much ignored her.

"Oh, it's only Laurie," one said to another one day, right in front of Laurie and Kristin. Terribly hurt, Laurie ran away.

Another time, a slightly older boy asked her to "go with him." When she turned him down, he ran off and shouted back at her across the track, "They dared me to do it!"

Big joke on poor Laurie.

As she watched Kristin interact with others, Laurie realized that she, too, had a lot of love for people. If only she weren't too scared to let them know it.

After Laurie's eighth grade graduation, our whole family was caught up in an exciting project, when we had bought our big, just-retired, diesel-powered school bus, and began remodeling it. All of us worked together doing body repair, sanding, painting, paneling, carpeting the interior, putting in appliances and bunks, and on and on.

Tom and I believed that we needed to spend a year of quality time with our four girls. They had shared us with many other people for a long time, and they needed to know how special they were to us.

We planned to leave shortly after the beginning of the next school year, when Laurie would be in the ninth grade. We withdrew the girls from school and found correspondence courses for them.

Our bus project had been exciting at first, but that year turned into a nightmare. To make a long story short, we ended up in terrible financial trouble, and had to choose between our bus trip and our house. After much prayer and soul-searching, the whole family unanimously agreed that God wanted us to take that trip, so we went ahead with our plans.

But the year dragged on, and delay after delay came along. Tom and I sort of went under for a while, wondering just what life was all about. Doubts and fears and confusion came in from every direction. We were half in, half out of the house. Finally Tom and I moved into the bus where we had many things to finish up. The girls stayed in the house with friends who were living there.

In hindsight I realize our girls had way too much unsupervised time. It was during this time that Laurie discovered that the boys were definitely noticing her. And, wonder of wonders, admiring boys could ease her feelings of inferiority and lack of confidence. She also discovered that in groups of people away from her former classmates, she could risk being herself. Even Kristin was amazed to see how Laurie related to her new friends.

Finally, the day we thought would never come actually arrived. After several false starts, we were ready to leave.

Kristin and her mom stopped to say good-bye. They were on their way to the doctor to check out Kristin's sore knee. "Bye, Laurie!" Kristin waved frantically as we drove out the driveway. "Have fun!"

God greatly blessed our year together as we traveled all over the United States and into Mexico, Guatemala, and El Salvador. It was a marvelous family experience, and worth every bit of struggle and sacrifice.

At the beginning of our odyssey we spent several weeks in Colorado Springs with friends. One day, as the girls were doing homework, the phone rang. It was Kristin, and she wanted to talk to Laurie.

"Hi!" Laurie exclaimed, surprised and delighted to hear from her. "What's goin' on? How are you? I was just thinking about calling you."

I was standing near Laurie while she talked to Kristin. I remember thinking Laurie was awfully quiet. She and Kristin usually did a lot of giggling and clowning on the phone. But I happened to glance at her face and was shocked at what I saw. She was extremely pale and looked dazed. Her lips were colorless, and she leaned against the wall as she listened.

"What did you say they might have to do?" she asked. She held the receiver against her ear with both hands, then began crying and shaking uncontrollably.

I put my arms around her. "Laurie? What on earth . . . ?"

She stood holding the phone for a couple more minutes, then shoved the receiver into my hands and ran from the room.

Bewildered, I said, "Hello?"

Kristin's mother was on the line. "I'm sorry we upset her like this," she said. "Kristin called to tell her that the doctors have found cancer in her bone tissue. They think they might have to amputate her leg."

"Oh, no!" I pictured Laurie and Kristin running down the beach together or around the school track.

"Kristin was explaining how they plan to treat her with bone marrow transplants, chemotherapy, and so on. But Laurie was so upset that Kristin asked me to talk to her. I tried but I don't think I helped any."

We talked for a few more minutes before I said good-bye and went to find Laurie. She was on the living room floor, lying on her side, all doubled over and holding her stomach, still crying wretchedly. Her reaction was so extreme, it was almost as if she knew something the rest of us didn't.

What could I say? I held her, tried to comfort her, but she wouldn't be comforted. She cried for a long time.

I didn't say anything, but I was thinking, *Laurie, I know this is hard. Kristin is a beautiful girl and your best friend. But isn't it better for her to lose a leg than her life?*

Laurie wrote to Kristin as we traveled and received letters in return. Kristin looked on the bright side of things as she told about the various treatments she was getting. She was always encouraging, and Laurie seemed to be adjusting to the idea of her illness.

As we neared the end of our wonderful year, we heard that Kristin was in Venice. She wrote humorously about the crush she had on her doctor there, and told Laurie that she'd had her mother buy her a beautiful, new nightie so she could look her best.

Then, just a few weeks before we were due to come home, Laurie received a call from Kristin's sister. She said simply that Kristin had developed pneumonia in her weakened condition and had died.

"Oh, Laurie, she loved you so much!" she cried, and they wept together.

I was amazed at Laurie. She was sad, but she wasn't overwhelmed. Now I understood her reaction when Kristin had called the first time. Somehow God had given her insight, even subconsciously, and prepared her to receive this news without being devastated.

When we returned home, Lynn, Tia, and Dawn rushed to call friends. Laurie stayed in the bus. She had no one to call.

A few weeks after we'd gotten home, Kristin's mother came to see Laurie briefly. She brought her a small box of photographs and letters, as well as an unfinished letter that Kristin had been writing to her. She also handed her the lovely, pale aqua, lace nightie that Kristin had worn in Venice.

Laurie was very lonely. She was sweet and thoughtful, but she wasn't happy.

When my brother got married, he asked Laurie if she would sing at his wedding. She agreed because she loved him but agonized over the thought of standing in front of all those people. We couldn't get her to believe what a beautiful voice God had given her.

Laurie became hysterical right before the ceremony, and though we were able to calm her some, she barely made it through her song. Obviously she still struggled with her lack of self-esteem.

She was too shy to put much effort into making new friends, though she desperately wanted them. When a young man named Terry reached out to her, he found her very eager for companionship. Sadly, Laurie lost even more self-confidence in that relationship.

Terry was strong and outspoken. He took her to glamorous places, gave her extravagant gifts, and was fiercely possessive. He obviously cared for her, but he didn't know how to treat her like a real person. She was a woman to be pampered, taken care of, and defended. He was the giver, she nothing more than the one who needed all he chose to give.

We watched helplessly as Laurie seemed to age before our eyes. Terry was a lovable person, and we, like Laurie, were all very drawn to him. But we could see the potential for great hurt to both of them.

At first Laurie didn't want to hear our warnings and concerns. After all, he was her friend, someone to lean on. Gradually she began to see that something had to change. She was extremely unhappy, quiet, and withdrawn.

Not only was Laurie's view of herself deteriorating, so was the way she related to God. She longed for the days when she'd been able to respond to Him freely and lovingly. Now she felt so small and insignificant that it seemed as if she couldn't matter to God anymore.

Laurie tried to cut off her relationship with Terry several times, but breaking up hurt so much that she backed down each time. Besides, if both Kristin and Terry were gone, who would she have for a friend?

When the break was finally made, it was an excruciatingly difficult, wrenching experience. One day she came to me in tears.

"Mom," she wept, "I feel like God is going to take away everyone who means anything to me!"

At the same time she became very tender toward God, and longed to know what it meant to really trust Him. She wrote in her journal:

> I know now that I can't depend on my friends for my happiness. I have to depend on you, Lord. You are so good and kind to me. I feel like all I can do is take and take. I want to GIVE you something. What can I give? My life? It's in your hands, Lord. Mold it, shape it, but gently please.

Laurie began to understand that she was a unique individual. She started to like herself more. Then she gradually discovered that other people liked her, too.

She soon found herself part of a close group of friends in her high school. She grasped these friendships eagerly. They were truly very special people, but all of them, like her, were busy trying to discover their own identities at this point of their lives.

Laurie's senior year and the summer that followed were filled with glamour and excitement. There were parties, dances, happy times rushing here and there, lots of fun with lots of people.

When she talked about Rick, a new friend she had met at her senior prom, there was a sort of a glow. She started spending a lot of time with him. As the weeks passed, the shine faded a little. Her smile wasn't so spontaneous anymore.

She worked with her closest girlfriend, Kim, for a home-cleaning agency. Transportation from home was complicated, and Kim had a car, so sometimes she stayed at Kim's house because it was closer to work.

We saw very little of Laurie that summer. When she was home, she seemed restless and in a hurry, though she was always very loving. I had the impression that her life had sped up to a frantic blur, and I found myself wishing for September to come.

Laurie had decided during her senior year that the fall after graduation she would go to a Bible school in another state. She knew that the people who were accepted at this school were really serious about life, and she also knew it would be a tough change after her whirlwind summer.

It wasn't a glamorous place. There was no beautiful campus or entertaining program. One of the main goals of this school was to give students a quiet place away from the noisy clamor of the world. There they would have time to think and learn and give themselves a chance to establish a foundation for the rest of their lives.

Also, while living in apartments with each other, they would have to learn to relate to one another with understanding and love.

This rigorous life was what she wanted. Underneath the fast pace her life had assumed, she had one constant desire. She wanted to know God. And she became more and more certain that she had to get away to give herself breathing space.

None of us knew then just how much she needed that space.

Several times in the last weeks before Laurie left, she expressed her fears about leaving home. I thought she was simply anticipating how much she would miss all of us, especially Carina. Then I began to pick up on a strange note in her remarks.

"I'm just afraid I won't have any friends when I come home," she told me.

Another time she said, "I feel like I'm walking away from everything and everyone I love. I'm scared."

I started to gain a little understanding of the desperation I'd observed in her frantic running around.

One day, shortly before she left, Laurie and I were in the car. I glanced at her solemn face and decided to ask her the question that had been forming in my mind for several days.

"Laurie, I've been wondering. You seem very fearful about leaving. Does your fear have anything to do with Kristin's death? You left for a year once before, and when you came back, Kristin was gone."

Her eyes widened, startled. Then the tears came. I had my answer.

At the airport a few days later, I held my breath. I knew how hard it would be for Laurie to board that plane. Besides Tom, Lynn, Tia, Dawn, Carina, and me, Kim was there to see her off. And, of course, Rick was there.

We all cried as we said our good-byes. I looked the other way when she gave Carina one last hug. Then she said good-bye to Rick.

It was especially hard for her to tell him good-bye. I had the distinct impression that she knew this was good-bye for good, not just to Rick, but to the whole way of life he represented.

Laurie walked toward the open door to the ramp, then turned back, and came to me. Tears streamed down her flushed cheeks. She clutched a single, red rose.

"Mom, I don't think I can do it!"

How I wanted to call it all off and take her home again. But I told her, "Sure, you can, honey," and gave her a gentle shove toward the door. She slowly walked a couple of steps, took a big breath, squared her shoulders, and marched down the ramp without looking back.

Our first call from Laurie was a tearful one. After the plane trip she'd had a long bus ride. When she finally reached the school, she found things in chaos. The apartment complex she was to live in was being remodeled and hadn't been finished on schedule. In her apartment the rug wasn't installed yet, and the plumbing wasn't finished.

"And, Mom," she sobbed, "my boxes haven't arrived." We had mailed them ahead, and they contained most of her clothes and all of her bedding and earthly treasures.

"Besides that," she went on between sniffs, "the building the school is supposed to use won't be available for a few days. We had to have registration in the parking lot. Last night I borrowed a sleeping bag and slept on the floor with ten other girls in one of the finished apartments."

My heart was urging me to say, "C'mon back home, honey!"

Then she said, "I was going to call and tell you I was coming home, but I found out that other people feel just as lost as I do. I think they will be good friends." She managed a little laugh. "I guess I'll survive."

I wasn't so sure when the next day her boxes were delivered to us at home instead of her. With a sigh and a prayer I sent them off again.

The letters we began to receive were full of ups and downs, but basically Laurie was toughing it out. She was very excited about her new friends, and we breathed the sweet air of relief.

Then came the phone call.

4
ON HEARING GOD

At first it seemed unthinkable to let Laurie stay in school for the rest of the semester. How was she ever to handle all that was ahead of her on her own? She had so many huge decisions to make.

The first decision regarding abortion was already made. But her decision for a full-term pregnancy did bring up other critically important questions.

Where would she go for prenatal care? I'd always made all her doctor and dentist appointments for her up until now. But she would have to investigate the possibilities herself this time and in a town where she knew no one to help.

And what about the baby? Would she keep it or give it up for adoption? The fact that marriage to Rick wasn't an option for several reasons would definitely affect her decision about whether or not to keep the baby.

My own emotions came through loud and clear on this issue. This was my first grandchild! A precious baby to love. Someone for Carina to play with—the little brother or sister that she'd probably never have any other way. After all, I was forty years old when we

31

were surprised with Carina. I'd been five months pregnant with her when we had returned from our bus trip.

We could always make room for one more. Our friends would provide a wonderfully understanding and supportive atmosphere in which to raise the child. Both Tom's family and mine would be loving and kind and would receive the baby well, though they would need some time to accept the situation. We would have to work through the what-will-people-say question with them, but I was sure our relatives would find grace to cope with their feelings.

I knew, too, that Laurie would be an excellent mother. She and two-year-old Carina were extremely close. In fact, leaving Carina behind was one of the hardest things about going away to Bible school.

I could get really excited, but at the same time I knew I had to be realistic. With Carina's recent birth I was all too aware of what it was like to be a new mother. I'd already raised three children and also had the support of a wonderful husband. Even with these advantages, it was hard work.

Initially, Laurie wouldn't have to worry about a place to live or the finances involved in taking care of herself and her baby. We would figure out a way to make room and provide for both of them. But I knew my daughter well enough to understand that before long she would be struggling with many things.

She wouldn't feel right about simply being cared for, along with her baby, as part of our household. No matter how much assurance we could give her that she wasn't a burden, she would want to pay her own way.

If Laurie went to work, I was more than willing to take care of her baby. But she knew I got tired already as a forty-two-year-old new mother. Was my stamina up to another little one? And how would she react if her baby started calling me Mommy?

Then there was the fact that she wasn't trained for a job that could support her and a child. Even if she found a good job, scarce in our area, rent was atrocious. If she tried to hire a babysitter, much of her wage would be immediately consumed.

And what about her social life? All her friends were still free of the responsibilities she'd have. She wouldn't be able to go whenever and wherever they wanted. I was afraid she would withdraw and pour all of her energy into her child.

Then there was Rick. I was pretty sure that if she kept her baby, she'd be seeing a lot of him. After all, the baby would be his, too. How would Rick's influence affect Laurie? How would he affect the baby as he or she grew, especially in the teen years?

And there was Rick's family to consider. They were also the baby's grandparents, aunts, and uncles. They'd want to be part of the baby's life and have every right to be as involved as they chose.

I became more anxious as I considered the reality of it all.

There was also the issue of Laurie's future husband. How would he feel about her baby? Would he be able to accept the child as readily as the children that would be born into their marriage?

I recalled the girls that Tom and I had counseled. Some girls had kept their babies. We'd watched the children grow, and sometimes we saw resentment on the part of the mothers and a lack of discipline. On the other hand, there had been cases where this scenario had worked out well.

I thought of adoptive parents I knew. What an unspeakably precious gift was theirs in the new baby that finally came after years of aching and waiting, hoping and dreaming. On the other hand adoptive parents weren't perfect either.

If Laurie decided to give her baby up, I knew the emotional agony involved would be tremendous. If I had a hard time even thinking about letting go, how would Laurie be able to do such a thing?

Painful though it was because of what it might mean to us, I found out all I could about adoption. In the intervening years, adoption laws have changed, so understand I'm speaking here of the laws as they were at the time of Laurie's pregnancy.

I had heard of something called independent or private adoption, sometimes dubbed "brown-market" adoption. Frequently a doctor or lawyer initiated or oversaw the process at the request of the mother, bypassing an adoption agency. Independent or private adoption was legal as long as it was carried out in accordance with state law. The biggest drawback was the lack of a buffer between the birth mother and the adoptive family.

On the other hand, there was an excellent adoption agency in our city. The agency would stand for the child, protecting his interests not only in his placement but also in all the required legal dealings. This advocate for the baby was often the missing piece in private adoptions. I knew our local agency would do an extensive home study both pre- and post-adoption to ensure the baby's well-being. They offered much prayer and showed great concern in their careful and considerate search for homes.

If Laurie chose adoption, she would be able to have a say in the choice of a family for her child. There were many couples who had been on the waiting list for years. The agency would provide a complete description and evaluation of the prospective families—everything short of their name and location. Laurie could decide which family was the one she saw as best for her baby.

In our state at that time the natural parents signed a release, and at birth the baby was placed in the custody of the adoption agency. In most cases, the adoptive parents could pick up the newborn at the hospital.

From then on, the child was the responsibility of the agency until the adoption was legal; then the adoptive family would be fully accountable. Until the legalities were final, the agency could remove the child from a home that proved unfit. In a closed adoption like this, the natural parents relinquished all rights to their baby and gave up the privilege of contact with the child.

Oh, that was so final. My heart ached, anticipating the pain Laurie would have to work through if she went the adoption route.

Emotionally speaking, it was obvious that the easiest thing, at least at first, would be to keep the child. I understood why most of the girls who carried their babies to term did keep them. But I strongly suspected that many unwed mothers who decided to keep their babies actually had made no decision at all.

Also, for many of those girls, the reality of colic and dirty diapers didn't occur to them before the birth of their babies. They thought of a soft, cuddly person who would love them and keep them from being lonely. But thanks to Carina, Laurie knew what it was like to have a baby in the house.

Beyond all of the reasoning and uncertainties was yet another basic question: Was adoption even a valid consideration? What did the Bible have to say about it? Did it really give any concrete instruction, or was it silent on the issue? Or was adoption, like so many other things, subject to one's personal interpretation or application?

In my Bible reading, I found that the New Testament certainly speaks of adoption in a number of places in a very positive light! Ephesians 1–5 says that ". . . In love he predestined us to be adopted as his sons through Jesus Christ."

I was all too aware of the way that people scraped and dug around for verses to back up convictions they already had and didn't intend to let go. Then, of course, there were always others who could come along and use Bible passages to "prove" the exact opposite. I didn't want to play that game.

Ultimately, all that really mattered was that Laurie discover what God's plan was for her baby and herself. Only He in His great wisdom could know what was right for both of them.

Bible school was a good place for her to listen and hear what God was saying. None of us doubted that God would let His plan be known.

Because Laurie expected God to answer, she had many times in her own experience heard the quiet, gentle, but persistent voice of God. She knew He wouldn't leave her to lean on her own wisdom. This time, more than any other time in her life, she was sorely in need of the peace and assurance that comes from knowing that the right decision is made.

She needed to carefully consider every aspect. The final decision as to whether to keep her baby or give it up for adoption would probably be a process that would continue throughout most of her pregnancy.

There would be many pressures as the decision about Laurie's baby was made. These pressures would not be just on Laurie, but on us, too. There would be emotional pressures, but even greater would be the pressure to make a "logical" or "reasonable" decision, one that might not coincide with God's best.

5
DEAR LAURIE . . .

Lord, give me Your words for her. I wanted every word to be perfect in that important first letter.

Dear, sweet Laurie,

I've done my share of crying since I talked to you, and I hurt. Don't get the idea that you've hurt me. I only hurt for you for lots of reasons.

First of all, it seems sad to me. News that could have been exciting and joyful under other circumstances was hard for you to tell me. You said, "I'm sorry." You don't need to be sorry for me, honey. I'm sorry, too. But not for any of the reasons you might think.

I'm not embarrassed or ashamed of you or afraid of what people would think if they found out. I'm certainly not mad at you, or thinking you're "stupid." I love you, probably more at this moment than ever before.

I'm sorry I can't be with you for the whole next seven months to encourage you and try to answer your questions when they come up. You have to make such big decisions and plans. You're going to be a mother so young, and you have such a huge job ahead of you. I was hoping you'd have a fairly care-free year.

Yes, I've been crying, but right now I can't find any anger in my heart toward God—only the opposite. I've found myself praising Him for what He is doing and what He will do in all of us.

I will support and stand behind any decision you make concerning the baby. If, after careful thought and honestly asking God for His plan, you believe He wants you to keep the baby, I will respect that. You must know that emotionally, my initial reaction is to fight to "keep" my first grandchild. YOUR baby. But I'm also trying to be as objective with you as I have been with other people's daughters.

One thing I think extremely important is the matter of guilt. Be absolutely certain that you don't have the idea that because of your sin, you DESERVE to HAVE to keep the baby, or to give it up for that matter.

Remember that you are dealing with a precious little life, and that you want to love that baby even more than with just a "mother-love." I know you want the very best for him or her.

God may show you that the very best would be a complete family. Through adoption your baby could grow up with the assurance of being desperately wanted. The child would eventually be told, "Your mother gave you up because she loved you too much to keep you. She was willing to suffer loss in order to give you the best."

You would be giving someone else the most wonderful gift in the world. You know, it's possible that someone has been praying for a long time and asking God for this baby. If God does ask you to give up the baby, He will give you the strength to do it. He can carry you through the moment when birth happens.

On the other hand, I know if you kept the baby you'd be a wonderful mother. Of course you could count on us for as much help as you needed, though we would respect your independence, too. Carina would certainly be excited!

Please understand. I don't know the answer, Laurie. I don't know what your decision should be. But, most importantly, there is one thing that you and all the rest of us have to do. We have to give this baby to God. Completely. Totally. He will determine the rest. He's promised that if you ask, He'll answer. He will give you wisdom because only He knows best.

I'm so thankful that you have the encouragement that you do at school. It's a wonderful place to be at this point.

Naturally, I'd love to be nearby, and I will be at every opportunity. But I entrust you to God's hands.

I'm proud of you, Laurie, and of the way you're able to accept your pregnancy. But don't feel like a failure when you have a weak moment now and then. The only true failure is the one who doesn't try. I love you.

Mom

As I was folding my letter, Dawn rushed up with an addition:

P.S. Hi, Lor, this is me, Dawn. I wish I knew
how you REALLY are. Do you want to know how
I felt when you called a while back and told us your
news? I knew you would. I cried. Why? Probably
for me, you, Mom and Dad, the baby, etc. Aren't I
selfish to worry about me? At school the next day
I was quite a space case. Everybody thought it was
because of the cross-country meet that afternoon.

That weekend I went to a Young Life camp and
learned quite a bit. One of the seminars was "What
to say to single pregnant women." I nearly jumped
out of my seat when I heard that.

There weren't very many of us there. The lady
that led it has been working in town with pregnant
girls for the last seven years. The main thing that
finally sunk in was that it's not an insurmountable
(that's the lady's word—no, I didn't think of it)
problem. It's not going to ruin anybody's life. That
made me feel much better.

I think God's going to teach you and the rest
of us some things that wouldn't be easily learned
otherwise. You'll have to ask Him what they are! I
couldn't tell you.

It wasn't many days till a letter arrived from Laurie. I hurriedly tore
open the envelope.

To my special Mom,

Your letter means so much to me. I've read it
over a bunch of times. Dad's phone call was wonderful, too. He was so loving. At first I could hardly
talk. I was so embarrassed and ashamed. I cried a
lot. But I did tell him that he wasn't supposed to
blame himself. I don't think he believed me.

I wish I weren't the cause of this dilemma. It
makes me sad to put such a burden on all of you. I

know you don't think of it that way, but I can't help being mad at myself.

I look at my situation with disgust. It's all so unnecessary. I wasn't so naïve as to not know what could happen, and I knew it was wrong. But I didn't care.

Your letter made me feel much more secure. I'm enjoying writing to you. Until I got your letter, I was afraid it would be uncomfortable, that somehow our relationship would change. But now I feel like we're closer, and that makes me happy.

The other day I ran into one of the heads of the school between classes. He knows I am pregnant and he assured me that the whole staff is behind me and wants to help. He said they definitely want me to stay.

But then he got pretty negative. I guess he wanted to make sure I was facing reality. He told me I'd go through this and that and to be prepared for the hard things I would have to face. I ended up feeling sort of discouraged.

That evening I prayed that Jesus would show me the joy He was going to give me. Somehow I knew He was going to use my circumstances for good. I prayed that I would be filled with His strength, peace, and joy.

Since then many things have happened! God has answered lots of prayers. I would hardly say, "I wish . . ." and it would happen. Just a lot of little things every day.

When you wrote that I needed to give the baby to God, I almost died. You see, the night before, I had been reading about Abraham. I read how God asked him to sacrifice the thing he loved the most—his son, Isaac. Then I realized that if I'm going to give this baby up (which I'm considering doing), I need to give it to God now. I have to know it's God's child, not mine. I can still love the baby, but not as my own.

I think it would be much easier to make it through my pregnancy if I knew I would be able to care for and love this child as a mother. As something that is mine.

At the same time a part of me feels stuck when I think of having a child at eighteen. I have felt from the very first that I should probably give the child up for adoption. I believe it was somewhat confirmed in my thinking last night.

Right now I am ninety-nine percent sure that God wants me to do this. But I need to be one hundred percent sure or I'll never be able to do it. That one percent of uncertainty is enough to keep me from making a decision. I've been praying for a very clear, definite assurance from God.

Everything you wrote to me was encouraging. Knowing that you have confidence in me gives me confidence in myself.

A day or so after I got your letter, I called Rick. I still needed to tell him that our relationship wasn't right and why. I had to ask him for forgiveness for letting it start, knowing that it could go nowhere.

Jesus gave me the words, and it was good. Rick wanted to understand me instead of fighting me. He didn't tell me I was stupid or selfish.

It wasn't terribly traumatic, because when I had said good-bye at the airport, it really felt final in my heart. It bugs me to think that our relationship could have been so much better. But it was easier just to let myself fall into the typical boy-girl thing. Oh that's a depressing thought.

Last Friday when I came home, there was a GORGEOUS bouquet of a dozen roses for me. They were from Rick. They were beautiful but it kind of made me sad.

Today has been pretty hard. I've been praying that God would give me the opportunity to tell the students here at school that I'm pregnant. I've had no guidance from anyone as to when and how, and I felt sure that it was time to bring it all out into the open.

Last night I just had this urge inside me to do it. I couldn't stop thinking about it, and it was driving me crazy. I wanted to let the girls in my apartment know, but I wasn't satisfied with telling just them.

One girl I had already confided in suggested that I do it in women's worship, when all the girls in the school are together. There is always a sharing time in those meetings.

On the way there I was so nervous and afraid. I felt like they would all look down on me and talk about me behind my back. Then rumors would start, and pretty soon all the guys would be whispering about me, too.

But when it was time to share, I just made myself open my mouth. I said, "There's something I want all of you to help me with. I'm going to have a baby in May." Then I started to cry, and I said, "I really need you."

Everyone was very understanding and accepting. They didn't seem shocked or disgusted with me or anything. They were just loving and encouraging. God is so good to me. . . .

There were tears in my eyes as I finished reading Laurie's letter. How I wished that she weren't forced into making such difficult announcements, such big decisions. But I was very thankful that she still had plenty of time to make her final choice.

I felt that she was right to begin moving in the direction she was ninety-nine percent sure of. Inside I believed that she would eventually choose adoption. I knew I was walking into the teeth of pain to even think that way, but somehow it seemed right.

God would surely be faithful to change Laurie's course if that was what He wanted. Meantime it was my prayer that no one would try to tell her what to do. It had to be Laurie's decision. The best thing we could do was to help her become aware of all the details involved in either choice, then trust God to give her the peace and assurance she would need no matter what she decided.

6
"HE LOVES ME!"

At school, Laurie was learning much about decision making and finding God's will. She was also learning about true friendship and right relationships. There was one friend in particular that we began to hear a lot about. His name was Dave.

Dave had been blind for two years. His blindness, along with other serious physical problems, had been brought on by diabetes. Dave and Laurie were spending a lot of time with each other. Laurie said, "We feel like we have something in common: he's blind and I'm pregnant!"

Dave was one of those people who refused to let illness control his life. The diabetes had attacked his heart, liver, and kidneys as well as his eyes. He constantly lived with the possibility of death. But, incredibly, he was able to encourage and uplift others instead of demanding sympathy.

Looking at the picture of him that she sent home, I couldn't even tell he was blind. He was muscular and suntanned. He and Laurie often went jogging together.

Dear Mom,   October 13

You asked about Dave on the phone. Well, that's an interesting subject. I'm very attracted to him.

I don't know what to do about this problem! I don't know if I'm attracted to his looks, or if I'm only feeling a need for someone special at the moment. Maybe his physical condition gets to my heart.

Sometimes I think he looks at me as his little sister. Other times I know I'm something special to him. It's funny, we've never talked about it. We're probably both too chicken.

My problem is, I would love to be able to "claim" him. Not only for security, but because he's an extremely special person.

At the same time I don't need that kind of relationship right now. I have a feeling the next time I get real involved with a guy I must consider that it could be permanent. Otherwise, why get involved?

I especially can't let myself get caught up with anyone, no matter who it is, until my relationship with God is stronger. I need to learn how to trust Jesus, not humans. I need to know that God is my strength, my security, and my lover. Until then I can never be sure if what I'm feeling for a guy is really love, or if I am "loving" him with a selfish motivation.

I spend a lot of time with Dave. I spend more time talking with him than with Jesus. I don't want that! What will happen when we stop spending so much time together or someone else steps into the picture? I just want to know and love Jesus, and I think my feelings for Dave stand in the way. It bothers me.

I do trust Jesus, but not enough. It's hard to give my life to someone I can't see. He can't physically be here to hold me, talk to me, wipe my tears away. It's especially hard when there is someone who could do all those things, and I can see him! Even though he can't see me.

Anyway, Mom, just pray that I will know how to let go of Dave and trust God.

I don't want to put any expectations on our relationship. Then it would become selfish and I would ruin something good.

It sure helped to write all that out. There's one thing that confuses me. Is it wrong to need a human being? Or to want someone special to care about?

Before I had a chance to answer Laurie's letter, we got an almost hysterical phone call from her.

"Dave's leaving school! He's going home as soon as the quarter ends."

Laurie was extremely upset, and I wanted to board the next plane. Tom calmed us both down. He encouraged Laurie to hang in there, trust God for the outcome, and especially trust His wisdom concerning Dave. I waited until the next day, then wrote a letter.

Dear Laurie,   October 16

I got your special letter yesterday, not too long before you called. I only heard bits and pieces while you were talking with Dad. I probably don't have anything completely straight. Again, knowing how upset and lonely you were feeling, my first instinct was, "Oh, come home, Laurie!"

I didn't sleep well, woke at 4:00, and prayed a lot for you. I was asking questions that all started with, "Why . . . ?" You know. "Why does Dave have to leave? Why Laurie? Why? Why?" All I kept hearing in response were parts of that beautiful letter you sent me.

Remember the question you asked me toward the end of the letter? "Is it wrong to need a human being? Or to want someone special to care about?" My immediate response when I read it was, "Sure, it's okay to want someone special to care about as long as you don't need that someone in order to survive."

That's a question that all of us have to struggle with all of our lives. It's much too easy to depend on others for our happiness and well-being.

God has sent you there and He has begun something good in you. He will finish it, regardless of what (or whom!) is surrounding you.

You did say on the phone the other day, ". . . I'm thankful for such a beautiful bunch of people." I know it might not seem true, but there are more than a few people in that "bunch." You said a girl you didn't even know had given you a letter.

Oh, Laurie. I tend to get attached to a few special people really fast, like you do. Sometimes Jesus puts them in my life for just a season. I, too, often forget that they might not be there for keeps. I'm glad for your opportunity to learn that early.

I'm sure you've thought about what it would be like to be Dave's wife—all the hard parts as well as the lovely ones. I believe you could do it if God were to put you together. You could love him enough to handle whatever you had to, even his death. I must admit my heart about breaks at that thought. I want to protect you. But I also know that I'd love him, too.

One thing to remember is that you won't "lose" him just because he's leaving. God knows what He's doing. All of it is because He loves both of you. He is in control of any future relationship you might have.

Peace, honey! That's what I'm praying for. That's what Jesus wants to give you more than anything else. You know, "the peace that passes all understanding." You don't have to understand things in order to have peace.

Love you,
Mom

It seemed like a long time passed before I received an answer to that letter. I prayed continually that God would protect Laurie's heart. She was in such an emotional, vulnerable place. She would naturally want someone to lean on. Finally a letter came.

Dear Mom,   October 30

Wow, do I ever need to talk to you right now. I guess the best I can do is write this trauma out and hope it clears my thoughts. Do you ever feel like Dear Abby?!

I'm such a mental case I don't know where to begin. First of all, I am terribly "in love" with Dave. Now don't get me wrong; I'm "in love" with him, but I really love him, too!

We've been very honest about our feelings for each other. He likes me for me. It blows me away. He doesn't like me because he thinks I'm pretty. He can't even see me! He likes me and what goes on inside of me.

We share together, pray together, read the Bible together, laugh, and cry together. We've talked about things like kissing and holding hands and the problems that would present. We've talked about marriage. Not that that's what we're aiming for, but the possibilities are always there!

We have learned a lot and helped each other in our different (yet somewhat parallel) situations. We have grown individually and together in the past two months. Our relationship is centered in Jesus.

I always read all of Dave's assignments to him as my designated ministry here at school. For a while the staff didn't really know that we cared for each other. When they did see that our relationship was growing, they just said to be careful. I'm sure they can see how beneficial this relationship is to me because of the kind of person Dave is.

Since my last letter I've been learning to keep my focus on Jesus, not Dave. I've been spending more time alone, praying, and thinking. Jesus has been showing me how to find my security in Him.

I hope that gives you a clear picture. Now, here is the problem. Ever since we've been talking about our feelings for each other, we've gotten even closer. Those "special" feelings have grown. So, when we go out, or go for a walk, we hold hands or he puts his arm around me. This stirs up my emotions even more.

I like that physical contact. But I started feeling that our relationship was moving along a bit too fast and it began to scare me. God showed me that it wasn't right for those things to be a part of our friendship right now. I feel that by acting this way we are making an unspoken commitment. I'm just not ready to do that yet.

I don't think the special feelings we have for each other are wrong. I'm free to love Dave and be close to him. I don't have to feel guilty about it like I did with the other guys I went out with. For once in my life I can honestly say it's okay.

If our relationship is going to grow, then I want to let it grow. But I don't want to push it along by a physical closeness, even though I love it! I've never made such a big deal out of holding hands or having an arm around me. It almost seems stupid! But our relationship is very important to me. I want to do things right for a change.

The reason I'm so bugged is that last night we had a long talk about it. But I couldn't express my feelings to him. I got all confused and couldn't come right out and say everything I just told you.

I was up to my old tricks again. I knew what God was pointing out to me, but I was afraid to say it.

I started expressing myself in a roundabout way, causing confusion in both of us. Also I knew that if I told him what I was thinking, I'd have to let go of all the "good feelings" of being held or holding hands. I just couldn't sort my thoughts and feelings out.

Dave knows how to express himself really well. He's not afraid to say much of anything. His openness encourages me to be open, but his ability to talk intimidates me. I feel like I could never express things as well as he does, so I become filled with fear when I know I have to communicate something.

Not only am I afraid of being open and making myself vulnerable, I'm afraid nothing will come out right. And it doesn't. My mind goes blank, and I get confused. So Dave ends up practically digging things out of me. Luckily, he's very perceptive and sort of figured out what I was trying to say.

It made me feel sick inside. First of all, I'm not sure that he understands totally, because it didn't come directly from my mouth. Second, it's not fair to him. He does most of the talking, while I sit and listen, and comment here and there.

Things were really tense between us at school today.

Next Day

I read this letter to Dave last night. I feel much better. Things are finally clear between us!

Lately I've been praying that God would heal me in the area of communication. I told Dave that I often feel like I'm stupid and can't talk. I think this goes back to some previous relationships.

The hardest time for me to be open is when it has to do with a person I care about. I can't express my feelings about that person or about a problem we're having.

It's hard for me to talk about this. It's hard to admit to anyone (even a mom or dad sometimes) that you have a weakness. One of the reasons I came to this school was to get rid of all those old hurts and fears. I want to be released from them and be free to be me.

This week we've been studying self-acceptance. It is the best teaching we've had yet.

Our teacher used the illustration of Adam and Eve and how they covered their "sins" (nakedness) with fig leaves. We use fig leaves to cover our hurts and frustrations, but they always pop up again. He was saying we need to rip those fig leaves off and let Jesus heal us.

Last night was like ripping a fig leaf off. I don't think I've ever been so open with a guy in my entire life. God has used him in many different ways. I know this is just the beginning of a healing God is doing in me. It's beautiful. I feel so much more free to be me.

Well, I could go on forever, but I have to get this in the mail. Please write as soon as you can. I really need to hear your opinion on our relationship and what's going on. Do you think it's wrong, right, good, bad? Do you see areas that should change between us that I don't see? I love you. Writing

to you always seems to help me get my thoughts
straightened out.

Love and kisses for all!
Laurie

Unexpectedly, Tom and I were able to fly south on business, and
we saw Laurie for a much-too-short visit. But it helped to know that
we very possibly would be back down for as long as a two-month
stay while Tom worked with his nephew. Laurie was ecstatic in anticipation. We would bring the bus and Carina. Tom and I would be
nearby during a time when she really needed the extra support.

We met Dave and visited for a short time while at the school apartments. On the way home I wrote to Laurie.

November 9

. . . As I said before, our encounter with Dave
was much too brief, but we'll get to know him better later.

I've been thinking that you're really right to
postpone making any serious commitments and
plans. As you said yesterday, you're very emotional
at the moment. You'll continue to be for some time
yet. Even after the birth.

Your feelings of being "misfits" together are
fairly temporary, as you know. Although I believe
God has given you to each other for encouragement
right now, take it one day at a time. Wait until you
can both be much more objective before you start
thinking marriage. Maybe that is God's plan, but
it's not your priority now.

Don't misunderstand. If, at the right time, God
were to make it clear that Dave is the man for you,
I would be excited and happy and supportive. I'd
know He would give you all the strength you'd need
for such a marriage . . .

The end of the quarter came, and Dave went home. Soon Laurie received a letter from him. She wrote to us of her response to his letter.

> ". . . He does nothing but encourage me. He tells me he prays for me all the time. One thing shows me more than anything how much he cares about me. He's so concerned about my relationship with God. What he wants more than anything is for me to have a close, intimate relationship with Jesus. It's neat because I feel the same about him. Anything else is second to that . . ."

7
GROWING PAINS

Before we knew it, it was time for Laurie to come home for Christmas. We were now living in our bus, and Carina was ecstatic about Laurie's return.

"Laurie's gonna sleep in Laurie's bunk, isn't she?" she would ask daily.

Laurie wanted our close friends and family to know that she was pregnant before she arrived. She was now secure enough in her relationship with the Lord that she felt she could handle the what-will-people-think issue. I thought sharing her news was a very good idea and would save lots of difficult and embarrassing moments.

"She's about four months along, isn't she?" Tom sounded surprised when he thought how quickly time had passed. "She probably shows a bit by now, right?"

I nodded.

Tom groaned. "It'll be pretty tough to ignore, won't it?"

"Impossible, I'd say."

He crossed his arms, leaned back in his chair, and closed his eyes. Love welled in me as I watched him. I knew he continued to struggle some with "blame" that he wasn't a better father, that he hadn't somehow been able to prevent what happened even though Laurie assured him she didn't fault him.

Even as he struggled, I also knew he had developed a pretty solid sense of God's forgiveness. Ultimately, we were both able to receive that forgiveness for our own failures as parents.

But there was a great sadness about him that I couldn't understand, something that kept him silent in fellowship meetings, remote from close friends, even from me somewhat. But he was kind, gentle, and loving, and tried to explain.

"I can't put how I feel into words," he said one day. "I'm sure that I appear withdrawn, and in a sense I suppose I am. But I don't feel like it's a bad thing." He looked puzzled. "I've tried to check out my motivations. I'm not embarrassed. I'm certainly not ashamed of Laurie. I'm very proud of her courage, and the woman she's becoming. I'm not devastated by my own failure—though I still often wish I'd been more help to her."

He shrugged, arms outstretched, "What else is there? Anger? I'm not angry at anyone, especially God. How could I be when I see Him so skillfully using this thing in all of our lives?"

I smiled at him. "Watching you, I don't think that your silence is a negative thing either. I think you're still coming to terms with everything, and I know you're still struggling with guilt a bit. I understand that, because so am I. But that's changing."

Tom reached out and hugged me. "Just keep watching me! I don't want to pull inside of myself or neglect my responsibilities."

The following week we spent an evening with close friends. They, too, had noticed the change in Tom and asked him about it.

During the course of the conversation, Tom suddenly said quietly, "I know what it is. It's a sense of mourning that I am experiencing."

As we talked, it seemed comparable to the thing that King David experienced when the son that Bathsheba bore him lay dying. David knew his son was dying as a result of his sin in taking another man's wife, then having the man killed. He wore sackcloth and put ashes on his head while the child was ill. When the boy died, David washed himself and dressed, and went on with his life (2 Samuel 12:15–23).

"That's it," Tom confirmed the comparison. "I *am* in a state of mourning. I just didn't recognize it." He seemed relieved that he had solved the mystery, and our affirmation and understanding gave his emotions more validity.

Later as we drove home, we talked about it further. I remembered how we'd all felt when Laurie called.

"It was like somebody had died," I said.

"I guess I'm mourning several things," Tom said quietly. "I mourn the loss of our own child. She's had to move on into womanhood so early—so abruptly. I'm also mourning the possible loss of her child, our first grandchild, if she gives the baby up for adoption."

Many times I'd gone over that one in my own mind. How could any of us let this baby go? I knew that only God could give the strength and peace we would need if that was what He wanted.

Tom grinned wryly. "There's something else that's suffered a death blow, and I don't mourn it at all!"

I looked at him, surprised. "What's that?"

"Our pride," he answered simply.

Tom and I soon set about the job of telling everyone Laurie's news. Each time we confided in someone, it was a unique experience. We found that we could never quite predict the reaction.

The response that stands out the clearest in my mind came from Rhoda and Gary. They had been a part of our lives for years. We had known Rhoda as a child. Later Tom was one of her high school teachers, and she had lived with us after she graduated. After she and Gary were married, they lived with us briefly. We'd sort of been like Mom and Dad, and I guess we still felt some responsibility to be a good example.

Rhoda and Gary had a special relationship with our daughters and had spent many hours with them. Now they had four little daughters of their own.

Tom, Gary, Rhoda, and I sat sipping tea around their fireplace. Tom briefly told them about Laurie. Then he betrayed his own feeling of responsibility in the whole affair by adding sheepishly, "Now what are you going to do with me?" He slid down in his chair, eyes on the floor.

Gary didn't say a word. He stood up and walked quietly out of the room. A few minutes later he returned, carrying a basin of warm water, a bar of soap, and a towel. Setting the basin on the floor, he knelt, removed Tom's shoes, and gently washed his feet in the warm soapy water.

I immediately thought of Jesus, humbly washing His disciples' feet. They had protested vigorously. It was *they* who should be washing *His* feet!

I saw the Spirit of Christ in Gary as he showed us his love and acceptance so spontaneously. He carefully toweled Tom's feet dry, then came and washed mine. This time the tears were healing.

Most people we told about Laurie responded with empathy and understanding, at least in our hearing. No one cast any stones that we were aware of.

When Laurie came home for Christmas her pregnancy wasn't that obvious yet. She was a little uncomfortable at first, knowing that everyone knew. But family and friends, at least on the surface, seemed accepting and sympathetic and glad to see her doing so well.

Having Laurie at home made her pregnancy much more real to me. Occasionally I found myself wondering what so-and-so was thinking, or what others would think when they knew.

I understood that anyone who was already critical of us could look from a distance and say, "So much for the 'perfect' family."

It was all too easy to agree with our silent critics and discount anything positive that we'd ever accomplished in and by our lives. Thankfully we continued to receive great encouragement and support through faithful friends

Laurie wanted to give her baby the very best possible beginning in life. She was eating well, exercising, and getting regular medical care. She also planned on a natural delivery. She and her sisters had been present at Carina's home-birth, and Laurie had attended two other deliveries. While she was home for Christmas, she visited Inger, the experienced, well-respected midwife she had chosen to deliver her baby.

"Everything is fine, Laurie," Inger told her.

"The doctor gave me a May 13 delivery date," Laurie said.

"I think maybe a bit earlier," Inger said. "I think the first week in May."

Laurie also made an appointment with a woman from a highly recommended adoption agency. We met at a local restaurant, rather than in the downtown office. Pat was very patient and kind and answered all of our questions. She confirmed the things we had learned about agency adoption.

The main thing Pat stressed at the first meeting was that the final decision was, indeed, to be Laurie's. She assured us that there would be no pressure from them for adoption. They were glad to counsel girls through their pregnancies whatever their final decision turned out to be.

Christmas vacation passed all too quickly. We were a bit crowded in the bus, but it didn't seem to matter. We were together. It seemed that Laurie had hardly been there any time at all when she had to leave again.

After she returned to school I wrote to her.

> Hi, Sweetie,   January 3
>
> As soon as you give us the final word about whether or not you are staying down there next quarter, I'll start working on plans for getting down there to get you.
>
> Dad and I talked quite a bit about you yesterday. It was kind of special because, until yesterday, Dad hadn't really discussed your keeping the baby. But God has made some changes in his thinking. I think he wants to tell you about it himself . . .

Usually Tom talked to Laurie on the phone, but this time he wrote to her.

> Dear Laurie,
>
> Just some thoughts regarding last week's telephone conversation. You asked me to pray

specifically about what I thought you should do when your baby is born.

Before answering your question, let me describe my feelings since last fall. At that time you made it very clear that I was not to blame myself for your situation. A hard task. I constantly ask myself how I could have helped you more—given you more time, more support. I am extremely aware of my own sinfulness. The temptation has been very strong to condemn myself.

But there is forgiveness. For both of us. Either we are forgiven or we aren't. There is no "in between" place. Nothing partial or conditional. Our biggest problem is accepting God's complete forgiveness for ourselves. I pray that He will give us grace to receive His love and walk on.

From the first, adoption was the "obvious choice" in my mind. I've been seeing lately that my obvious choice has been based more on a "let's get it out of the way and get on with the show" mentality. There wasn't any significant insight into your needs or your baby's.

In the past weeks I've found myself trying to understand the impact adoption has on a child when he starts wondering what happened. Now I am seeing that the choice isn't easy at all. It is very difficult. The pros and cons abound. I feel ready to accept and support either.

In fact, I've been excited over the possibility of keeping the baby. This is the first time I've felt that way. Like I said, until lately, it's been only adoption on my mind. Of course, it was always couched in the framework of, "We'll support whatever decision you make."

There's another thing that I'm becoming aware of. I have been experiencing a sense of mourning that has led me to withdraw from a lot of things.

Maybe "non-involvement" is a better term than withdrawal.

The mourning is for you, for your baby, and for ourselves as we walk through this time together. There's no judgment, only repentance to walk in. "Joy comes with the morning" (Psalm 30:5 RSV).

I love you,
Dad

Laurie's feelings continued to rise and fall. One day when we called to see how she was doing, she was feeling very emotional about the baby and had been crying a lot.

"I can hardly wait for you to get down here for that job!" she said at one point, speaking of the job with Tom's cousin. "That's all that keeps me going at times."

That job did look like the perfect solution, putting us near Laurie at a time she needed us, but we'd had no word as yet.

After our telephone conversation, Laurie sat down and wrote us a letter.

Hi!   January 15

It was wonderful to talk to both of you yesterday. I didn't realize how badly I needed to. It was good for me to cry. I haven't wanted to keep the baby until recently. Yesterday I felt so overwhelmed by everything.

The fact that I'm pregnant is always there. I wake up in the morning, there's my stomach. I sit down to do homework, the baby kicks. I get dressed, my clothes look big and funny, etc. Then the other night I had a dream about the baby and I couldn't get it out of my mind. It felt like all the strength I'd had was gone. Everything seemed confusing, useless, and painful.

Then I got your letters and read what you wrote, Dad, about the decision to keep or give up the child being my decision. I really began to wonder if giving it up was or is of God. Or is it something I reasoned out?

All I want is God's will. I can't see what is in my future. I can't reason it out at all. No one can say what will be best for the baby or for me; we don't know! God is the one who is making the decisions and only He knows.

Right now I don't feel right about keeping it, although my emotions say, "Hang on to that baby!" But I still need reassurance. If God wants me to keep this baby, He'll just have to show me. I'm open to it.

Yesterday, after I got off the phone, I felt alone, weak, and sad. But as the day went on, the Lord reminded me of His goodness to me. I kept remembering things I had said, ways that He has changed me, promises He has made me.

I got two notes that day. One was from two guys thanking me for going to a movie with them and telling me they love me. The other was anonymous. It encouraged me and told me that I'm a display of God's strength. It said that I was becoming a beautiful woman of God and that I was loved.

I also remembered a statement I had made the other day. I was in a group of people, and I said, "If this is what it takes for God to bring me close to Him, to get me where He's wanted me for years, I don't mind the struggle. It's worth it."

A special verse I found says, "A woman giving birth to a child has pain because her time has come; but when her baby is born she forgets the anguish because of her joy that a child is born into the world" (John 16:21). That's the attitude I want to take.

All these things kept popping into my head. At first I kind of ignored them, but so many things had happened that I couldn't help but be encouraged. Then today in church I heard that "God won't give us anything that's going to crush us; He's always there to carry us through."

He loves us so much! I've just been overwhelmed by that lately. He sure takes good care of me. Yesterday could have been miserable, but instead He used it to strengthen me.

I still feel kind of sensitive and tender but stable and secure at the same time. I'm kind of going through "it" thinking about these next months, memories I'd rather not have, etc. But Jesus is taking me through it in His arms. He's healing, loving, and encouraging me. So keep praying. I still need it.

Next day, Laurie added:

I must send this letter, but, Mommy and Daddy, sometimes I feel so up and down I can't stand it. I feel so out of it today. Another one of those days I just can't handle. It's awfully hard to keep a positive attitude. I don't want to be pregnant; I don't want to have a baby. I don't want to give it away; I don't want to keep it. I have bitter feelings toward Rick. I want to come home!

I think I'd better quit. This is getting depressing. I'll hang in there. I'm just having a disgustingly rough moment or two. I love you lots and lots (all of you).

Bye Again,
Lor

It was very hard to read some of her letters. Typically, Laurie's feelings were very unstable, and I knew she probably felt quite differently by the time we received each letter. I often went to God for comfort or to vent my own feelings. Sometimes I resented the fact that she was being forced to mature so quickly. But usually I could see, as she could, God's loving, gentle hand in her circumstances.

Yes, Laurie was maturing into a beautiful young woman. And changes continued to happen in the rest of us, too. Our communication with each other was becoming more open as we all struggled with our feelings and shared them.

We were also finding out just what God's grace really was, both directly and through the love and acceptance of others. It was both humbling and strengthening as we shared our burden and exposed our family exactly as it was: human, weak, hurting, and entirely dependent upon God. Just like everyone else.

8
STRETCHING

"God, why is it that every time I think I've figured out what You're doing, You pull the rug out?" I complained. "Or did I just answer my own question?"

I couldn't help but cry. Plans for the job near Laurie had been delayed once again until after Laurie would be home.

"She'll probably decide to come home after second quarter now," I said. "I don't see how she can stay that far away from home as she gets close to term. This delay is the last straw!"

I was wrong. There was another "straw" waiting.

One wintry day, close to the end of January, the little cordless telephone in the bus started ringing. I picked it up, flipped the switch from "stand by" to "talk," pulled out the aerial and said hello.

"Hi. This is Kim."

"Oh, Kim! Hello!" Memories of Laurie's high school friendships came flooding into my mind. Kim and Craig, other members of the little group Laurie spent so many hours with, had visited her in the bus at Christmas time.

"How is school going?" I inquired lightly.

"It's OK. I just called to tell you that Craig was flying a light plane yesterday, and he crashed." Her voice caught. "He was killed."

I was stunned. That feeling again.

"He was—killed?" I managed. "Oh, Kim, I'm so sorry!"

"I wanted to know if you thought I should tell Laurie," Kim said. "I mean, would it be bad for her?"

The news would break Laurie's heart, but of course she had to know.

"Yes. She'd want to know. Go ahead and call her." After Kim told me when and where the funeral was, I hung up. Then, shaking, I dialed Laurie's apartment. She wasn't there, so I told the other girls what had happened and that Kim would be calling. I knew they would take care of Laurie. But, oh, how I wanted to be there myself.

I talked to her for a few minutes that night, and several days later I received a letter from her.

> Dear Mom,   January 24
>
> I just talked with you on the phone, and now I want to come home more than ever. I felt like there was so much I wanted to tell you, but I just couldn't get it out because I had *too* much to say, and I felt like crying. So I decided to write.
>
> When I heard about Craig's death, I couldn't understand it. I kept saying, "What are You trying to show me, Lord!?!" I kept thinking about losing Kristin and boyfriends, leaving this summer, Dave's leaving, then finding out you couldn't come down. So many feelings of loss or having to give up something important. And now, Craig.
>
> At the same time, I can hardly believe the things God's been showing me the past few days. He's been changing a lot of things in my life that I've been praying about all year. But it's happening so fast that I don't know if I can handle it.
>
> One of my prayers has been that I would be able to hear God's voice and know it's His. I've had

many special times talking and *listening* to Him. It's good to know I can go to Him anytime, anywhere, and He'll be there. He'll always come through, He'll always answer.

Last night I decided to go for a walk and pray. As I was walking, Jesus asked me if I would be willing to give my family to Him. I realized that I was afraid to. He said, "Laurie, I want all of you."

I knew then that I haven't been giving Him everything. I haven't been willing to go anywhere or do anything He wants. I've been saying, "Lord, just do what You want with my life." But when He would ask me to do something hard, I'd say, "No way. God couldn't expect me to do that."

As I kept walking He showed me that my holding back had to do with the baby, too. At this point I was still wondering what He wants me to do, and wanting confirmation.

Mom, I had been praying, "Lord, soften my heart, open me up to Yourself." The minute He showed me how closed I had been, I could confess it and my attitude changed.

Then within the next couple of days He showed me that I wasn't willing in my heart to give Him the baby. I've been saying, "Sure, no problem. God can help me face an adoption if this is what He asks me to do." But I wasn't really willing.

I didn't know how to change. I was about to go crazy. I didn't know how to pray about the future for the baby or myself.

So here I was at the *end* of my rope, and I got a letter. It was from a friend who had a baby before she was married and kept it.

The main things she said were: 1. Don't be afraid to love your baby whether you keep it or not. 2. God will *show* you if you're to keep it; if you're to give it up, He'll give you strength. 3. Don't feel like your baby's a sin. 4. Whatever you do, do it in love.

I didn't really know how to apply it all to myself, but I knew it was from God. So I went for another walk to be alone with Him.

I said, "OK, talk to me," but my troubled little brain wouldn't calm down. Then, in between thoughts, I heard this gentle voice: "You don't trust Me." I realized it was true and started crying.

I *know* He loves me; I *know* He doesn't want to see me hurt; I *know* He has the power to bring me through even an adoption, if that is His will. But I couldn't trust Him.

All I could see was that I would have to let go of something, and I remembered the hurts I've felt in the past. Only this seemed to top them all. I kept imagining myself going through the birth—and then the baby's gone.

I sat in a playground alone for a long time, just thinking about what it would be like. I'm a mommy and I'm never going to know my baby. I cried a lot and it felt good.

I believe that God is asking me right now to give the baby up. If He wants me to keep my baby, He'll tell me and I'll know for sure. But right now I'm sure of what He is saying to me. Does it ever feel good to *know* He's spoken to me, not only through Scripture and through people, but one on one! It's such a peaceful feeling.

This is just the beginning. I don't really know how to trust Him. But He'll guide me and teach me more and more each day.

Next Day

Sometimes I love it here and feel good about being here. But other times I'm ready to pack my bags and leave. These negative feelings are getting more and more frequent. I get *so homesick.*

I can't handle early hours, lectures, homework, finances, or people. I wish I were home where I could relax and be understood. My brain is getting pumped full of Church history, Bible readings, books, and studies. All this on top of everything I am learning in my personal life. I might go nuts.

And, I'm pregnant and no one really understands what I go through. I want my own home with my daddy and sisters and I want my mommy! Wah!

Lately I feel so exhausted all the time and my tummy hurts. I have a sore throat today and my head aches. My insides aren't feeling so hot either. I almost threw up this morning.

I don't know why, but I can't seem to get the things done that I want to do in a day. So I push myself. I know I should take naps, but I don't have time. And now I'm sick, too.

I really wonder what I'm doing here. Mom, is it stupid for me to stay? Part of me wants to stay and get to know people better. I want to learn more, become more independent, and grow stronger. I spend more time alone with God in this situation.

Then the other part of me says, "God won't quit teaching me just because I'm home."

I'd love to bring that tuition money back to you.

But then, it would be nice to have only one and a half months of pregnancy left when I get home. And it will be fun when you come to visit.

I guess I need to pray about it.

Later:

Well, I did. And I do believe I'm supposed to stay. But it's so hard sometimes. I stayed home from school today and I feel rotten. I'm not going tomorrow either. When I feel better physically, I'm sure I'll feel better about being here.

I really hope you can come down for a visit. But if it's too much of a strain financially, I understand. Lately I feel so much pressure about money, because I imagine you are probably pressured. Especially Dad. Neither of you has said anything about it at all. I just get so frustrated because I know we aren't rich, and I seem to use so much money. I'm learning to be more careful when I shop, but everything costs a lot.

Well, enough of this sickening subject.

I could talk to you forever, but I need to go to sleep. My head's killing me and the glands in my neck are swollen. It hurts, Mommy! I feel like I'm going to kick the bucket!

So I think I shall say good night. I love you and the rest of my dear family. Take care—

Love,
Laurie

P.S. Mom, I feel so nervous because I haven't had any childbirth classes. Could you ask Signe if she would teach me some stuff when I get home? I know Inger is my midwife, but Signe is one, too, and she is such a close friend. She's had so much experience training mothers and delivering babies.

I carefully folded the letter and put it back into its envelope. That took some concentration, because my eyes were blurred with tears.

My feelings were mixed. I was glad that Laurie had three more months to make her final decision. But, at the same time, I fervently wished that it was all over. The see-sawing emotions and decision-making process were overwhelming to me sometimes. How much more difficult it must be for my little girl.

But this was no way to be thinking if I was going to answer her letter. So I pulled myself together, wiped my eyes, blew my nose, and sat up straight.

I began by writing the usual motherly concerns about her swollen glands and all her aches and pains. Then I had an interesting thought.

> . . . You know, Laurie, I think I know one of the reasons I don't get to come flying to you right now. If I did, we'd probably enjoy being together so much we wouldn't talk nearly as thoroughly as we write. Know what I mean? I've appreciated your letters tremendously.
>
> Some people seem to have no comprehension of what I'm talking about when I say I need to know what God wants concerning coming down there. After all, you want me to come, I want to go, we *could* get the money together, so what else is there to consider? The idea that God might not *want* me to go right now is unfathomable. . . .
>
> Well, my dear, I'm sure you know, and I can't really tell you how much, I want to be with you. I get an ache in my heart quite regularly when I think about you. But I also have peace.
>
> People hear of your struggles, see me cry, and can't understand how you can say, "It's OK." But we know, don't we? God will have everything His own way and it will be best.
>
> I was so glad to read about the peace God is giving you concerning the baby. It's quite a process, isn't it? We're going through another process of our own. This has been especially difficult for Dad, as

he explained to you in his letter. We are both totally willing for the decision to be made either way.

Lynn and I are getting awfully excited about our planned trip down there. Lynn has two full weeks of vacation. We can come and spend most of a weekend with you, then go visit Grandma until it's time to bring you home. I can't believe that you have already been down there for almost three quarters. Time has flown in spite of the fact that I miss you so much.

By the way, I talked to Signe. She says don't worry about your lack of childbirth classes. She'll be glad to teach you all you need to know when you get home. She assured me that six weeks is more than ample time. (Carina is sitting on my lap "dancing" to some music. Makes it really easy to write!)

Are you still having some thoughts about staying down there fourth quarter? I guess my big question would be whether you can physically handle it. If it were me, I don't think I could, but maybe you feel different than I did when I was pregnant.

You really should be getting naps and not staying so tired. Don't I sound like a mom? Well, my dear, you are the only one who can decide when to come home.

I must quit. Consider yourself hugged. I love you.

Mom

9
UPS AND DOWNS

Dear Mom,   February 18

It's Saturday morning and I'm sitting on the living room floor feeling quite useless. I don't feel good physically either. I came home from school early yesterday. I think I've been in this very same place ever since, except to move to the kitchen table now and then.

My stomach was real hard all day yesterday, and low, in a big, round ball instead of being all spread out. I feel like I have cramps and I'm weak. I want to go out and do something, but my tummy hurts. If I don't get off my rear end and move, I'm going to turn into a large piece of lard. I want to go out for a walk, but this is our first day of rain in two weeks. Besides, I don't know how far I'd make it.

Mom, it's so easy for me to hide. Sometimes I don't like being around people outside of my apartment. I feel awkward. My stomach gets in the way. I know people accept me as I am, but I can't really be me. Not just because of the mental part of it all, but the physical, too. I get tired so easily and my body hurts. I hear people running around outside, being silly, doing crazy things. It's hard to explain how I feel.

Thursday night a guy asked me if I would go to a concert with him and some others. I knew I needed to get out, so I went.

I had a good time, but I still felt kind of funny. The two other girls that went are real skinny and pretty. They were all dressed up in their high heels and straight-leg jeans. One of them looked at what I was wearing, laughed, and said, "Oh, you look so . . . cute!"

I felt like a blob. I just can't get away from it! I want to be normal. I want to be able to go out with my friends and not feel so self-conscious. Do you understand? I've never sat around so much on weekends in my life. It's not that I never do anything. It's just that if I weren't pregnant, I think I'd make more of an effort to build friendships and do things. I can't wait to be home. I feel lonely.

Well, I'm going to get up and around today. I'm tired of this. Sorry to sound so glum. I'm just frustrated from sitting so much. I think I need to put this letter away for a while and spend some time praying. All I want to do is come home right now and it makes me cry. I'll finish this tonight. I won't be busy, I'm sure.

Bye

Two days later

I'm back. What a sad morning that was! The rest of the day wasn't too bad. I just wasn't feeling like "me" all day. What a brat I was being! I don't think I was too pleasant to be around. I'm really beginning to feel *pregnant*!

Everyone at school always tells me how emotionally stable I seem. I just realized the reason I appear that way. I pour out all my feelings and troubles in letters to you.

It's nice to be able to do that instead of taking it out on everyone around here. Just don't you worry too much about the things I say. It's probably not as bad as it sounds.

Well, I've decided for sure to come home. I know I'll miss it here, but I feel good about leaving after third quarter, unless God shows me otherwise. So plan on it.

It's been raining hard all day. I was feeling like a piece of flab and couldn't bear to sit any longer, so I went out for an hour and walked in the rain. It was peaceful and relaxing and I had a neat time praying as I walked.

I've been reading some books that the doctor gave me. The more I let down my protective wall, the more I am able to let myself love my baby. I can pray for it and understand what I am feeling. It's such a release! I'm also starting to accept what's happening to me and what's going to be happening in the next couple of months. It's neat to know I can trust God, that He has it all in control.

Listen to this: "Now to him who is able to do immeasurably more than all we ask or imagine, according to his power that is at work in us . . ." (Ephesians 3:20). Even though I don't know how to pray, He's going to do more than I could ask or imagine anyway! Pretty groovy, huh?

I can't wait till you and Lynn and Carina get here. It will be so much fun! I feel different about seeing all of you, and about coming home. I'm more stable I guess—not so emotional about it all.

But I'm still just as excited. It's less than a month away!

Last night a bunch of us went out for dinner, then we went to a movie. I got tired and cranky about eleven o'clock. I just can't handle much these days. But don't worry. I've been taking naps when I need them.

Later

Oh Mom. Class was on abortion today. We had films. The first one was awful. I cried.

They showed a girl having an abortion. They put her out, but she screamed and her body went all shaky. They showed dead babies and all kinds of other hard things to look at.

This won't be an easy week of classes. I don't know that I can handle it. I sit for three hours and see films about babies. It gets to me after a while.

I love you guys so much. Thanks for being there. I can't wait to see you. You'll laugh when you see me. I look funny.

I must be going. I have to take my nap. I'm terribly tired.

Your lovely, shapely daughter,
Laurie

She had decorated her letter with a silly drawing. A pear-shaped girl stood looking down at her protruding tummy. It was hard to imagine my slim daughter with such a figure!

I didn't let myself dwell on what it must be like for Laurie to be watching films about abortion. But again I was so very thankful that she was watching them with a big tummy rather than having an extra load of guilt to deal with.

We all tried to keep mail going steadily in Laurie's direction. She was the envy of her roommates. She obviously held the record for getting the most mail!

Hi Mom,   March 1

Thank you for the cards, letters and package. They mean lots to me. Everything in that last letter was neat right down to the "I love you" on Dad's check. Carina's letter and picture made me cry. But never fear, they were tears of joy. I felt like showing the world all the stuff that was sent just to show off my beautiful family. I am so proud of you.

I can't wait till you get here! Only twelve more days! I can't believe how fast the time has gone. I only wish Dad and Dawn could come, too.

I'll actually be home in less than a month. I can see the timing is right as it gets closer.

In a way, I dread leaving here. It's been such a sheltered life with lots of intense learning. It's going to be hard stepping back into the real world, but exciting. I'm going to miss all of my buddies and all the time I've had to spend with Jesus. I know those times won't end, but it won't be so concentrated.

I can't remember if I told you how happy it made me to get Dad's letter and hear what God is doing in his life. It feels good to hear what *you're* learning instead of the focus always being on me.

I wish none of us had to go through this. At the same time I'm thankful for the way we're being drawn together as a family, the lessons that are being learned and the strength that is growing in all of us.

Five days later

I went to see the doctor today. I was emotionally and physically tired and didn't want to go in the first place.

The darn nurse wrote on my chart that my weight was 156 lbs. So when I saw the doctor, he tenderly informed me that I had gained ten pounds in three weeks and I now had gained a total of thirty pounds!

Actually I had seen that the scale said *146*, not *156*. I hadn't gained any weight at all. But I was so delirious I thought maybe I'd been seeing things. I tried to tell him that I couldn't possibly weigh that much. He only looked at me like, "Poor girl. Just humor her."

He said things like, "The baby weighs_____ and there's_____ much water and the rest you'll have off in no time." The more I tried to tell him the scale wasn't right, the more he tried to reassure me.

It was rather humorous, but I was quite flustered. Anyway, I've actually gained only sixteen pounds.

I think God's dealing with my vanity. I just got a letter from Kim. In it there was a picture of me in my bathing suit. I looked so skinny and tan; it made me ill!

I have such a hard time letting go of the past. I liked the way I looked, and now I feel as if I'm ruined. I'm afraid I'll have stretch marks and excess flab for the rest of my life.

Oh, it seems so silly. I've been too dependent on looks in the past. I want to be rid of all that. Maybe I'm just sensitive because I feel so awkward with this crazy stomach sticking out.

Yesterday at school, the secretary told me my stomach was beautiful because it is perfectly round and I carry it all out in front. She said there are lots of women who would love to look like I do when they're pregnant. It made me feel good.

I've been going for walks every night at sunset and praying. It's so beautiful that time of night. I love it. It's going to be hard to leave all this behind. I hope you're prepared for the mental case I may be when I get home. I hope you get this before you leave. I'm praying for a safe trip, and that Carina will be happy the whole way. I can't believe you will be here in a week! It was a month away just yesterday, it seems. (I'm writing with my tablet on my tummy. It's quite handy.)

I think the sun is affecting my brain, so I'll end this letter. See you soon!

Love,
Laurie

Laurie wasn't the only one looking forward to our trip. Lynn said she was getting teased at work for being so excited about taking a trip with *her mother*! Carina had talked about nothing else for days. I was so busy trying to get everything taken care of that I hardly even had a chance to think about being excited.

The departure date finally came, the car was loaded (was it loaded!), and Carina and I arrived at Lynn's job to pick her up. At the last minute Tom showed up from work to say good-bye. He looked so forlorn I thought he was going to jump in the car with us.

Miraculously, Carina was a wonderful traveler. Even when we got lost in the hills on the last leg of our journey, she was quiet and content in her bed in the back.

Laurie had almost given up on us by the time we finally dragged in. We were all so delighted to see each other that it took a while to get inside the door of her apartment.

She was right. We laughed at her. In fact we laughed a lot in the next few days. It was so good to be together. Laurie wrote to Tom after we left. We would be back to pick her up in a couple of weeks.

Hi, Dad,   March 18

Only two more weeks and I'll be on my way home! While Mom, Lynn, and Carina are gallivanting around down south, I thought I'd write. I've started quite a few letters to you that never got finished, so I think it's time I mailed one.

Mom and the girls took me away for the weekend. We had a wonderful time in our cozy little cottage in the redwoods. The best part was just being together. We spent most of the time sitting or lying around in our pajamas, just talking and laughing. We had such a special, relaxing time. (I've *never* talked so much in my life.)

Lynnie read to us, and Mom rubbed my aching back. Carina became my shadow. (She *never* stops talking!) I enjoyed the break from school with three of my favorite people. The only thing missing were my two other favorite people. I think I've fallen in love with my family.

Have you and Dawn been taking good care of each other? Enjoy the peace and quiet while you can!

It's a terrible feeling to desperately want to be home. I've waited and waited for the day to come. Now that it's almost here, I'm trying to drag out each day. I'm trying to take in as much as I can, dreading (in a way) the day I leave.

Sometimes I'm afraid to come home because it brings me closer to the birth of the baby and a possible adoption. When I get fearful, I start trying to prepare myself, trying to take the situation into my own hands. Then when I get thoroughly frustrated, I go to God and He always says the same thing: "Trust Me."

One day when I was praying, suddenly I saw that Jesus had been there all along, waiting for me to really trust Him. When I understood how patiently He had waited for me, something clicked inside me.

Now I feel so free in our relationship. Because of His love for me, I can simply love Him back. Not because I have to, but because I want to.

Before, I was doing His will and walking with Him because I *knew* it was best for me. I *knew* He loved me, and I *knew* I needed Him. It was a struggle; now it all comes so much more naturally, from within, because I love Him. It's like a whole new beginning.

Anyway, Dad, I can't wait to be with you and talk to you. I want you to know I love you. I'm happy and privileged to be your daughter. I feel like I tell you that all the time, but I have to tell you again because it comes from my heart.

Thank you for loving and accepting me as I am. I think the main reason I am walking with God today is the strong foundation that has been built in my heart throughout my childhood.

You gave me that start, my roots, in Jesus, not only by your words, but by your life. (Don't worry. I don't think you're perfect. So you don't have to live up to anything when I get home!)

Thank you for that foundation, Dad. It's the greatest gift you could ever have given to me. I appreciate you and thank God for you.

I love you.
See you soon,
Laurie

10
WAITING AT HOME

Lynn, Carina, Laurie, and I had a relaxing trip home. We had shipped most of Laurie's belongings ahead of us to give us more room in the car. We were joyfully greeted by Tom and Dawn. They had eaten enough Cheerios to last them a lifetime.

The first few days at home were spent sorting through Laurie's boxes and making room for one more person in the bus. Finally, we were finished and settled down to wait for the baby to arrive.

"It's so nice to have you where I can see you!" I gave Laurie a hug. "I must admit that it's a little hard to get past you in this bus though!" I laughed as she turned sideways to let me by.

She *was* beautiful pregnant. The secretary at school had been right. Her stomach was small and all out front. She didn't even look pregnant from behind.

"Mom, I'm so glad that even though things are the way they are, I can have a 'fun' pregnancy. I mean, we can laugh about my figure and the way I sit. Everyone isn't moping around or ignoring me."

Just then the phone rang. It was for Laurie. I went to the back of the bus to make our bed while she talked. Our bus was very elegant, and looked professionally decorated, but there still was no graceful way to make our bed.

I was on my hands and knees tucking blankets down the far side when Laurie came back there. It was her turn to laugh.

"I remember how you looked doing that when *you* were pregnant," she giggled.

I glared at her from under my arm. "You'd better be careful," I growled. "I'll make you do this."

Ignoring my warning, she tickled my feet and I fell onto my stomach. Bed making came to a halt as Laurie crawled onto it.

"Good phone call?" I asked.

Laurie frowned. "Yes, except I feel a little dumb when I talk to my friends. They all assure me that they are completely accepting, and I know they are. Everyone wants me to go out and do things."

She was lying on her back rubbing her tummy with both hands.

"Mom, I don't feel like it right now. I'm content to just stay home with you for a while. But when I tell people how I feel, they think I'm embarrassed or ashamed or something."

She pulled herself up on an elbow. "I guess they think if they can ignore the fact that I'm pregnant, I should be able to also." She looked at the mound on her middle and smiled weakly. "Kind of hard to ignore. It's always in the way."

"You only have another five or six weeks to go," I reminded her. Then, remembering that every one of my babies had been substantially overdue, I warned her, "Just expect to have to wait a little longer than the doctor says. Then, if you're on time, you'll be pleasantly surprised."

From time to time I felt a little uneasy knowing that Laurie still hadn't made her final decision about the baby. I wondered if maybe I should try to line up a bassinet and some baby clothes. But I knew how cruel that would be if she decided on adoption. I made myself trust God totally for the outcome. He is the God of detail as well as the God of big decisions. It was His responsibility to direct Laurie, not mine.

It wasn't too hard to hold to that trust, because Laurie didn't seem concerned about it. She obviously had confidence that God would come through all in good time.

Laurie and I talked on and on in the days that followed. One of the subjects that kept coming up was Laurie's deep concern for other girls in her situation. One day we were discussing a pregnant girl that a friend had told her about.

"She's a great girl, Mom, but she's having a terrible struggle," Laurie said. "I just have the strongest desire to go and see her and talk to her. Maybe I could help her a little, or be of some comfort or something."

"What's she struggling with?" I asked.

"Well," she answered, pulling Carina onto the bed beside her, "her family won't even acknowledge the fact that she's pregnant. Her dad won't look at her, and nobody will talk about it."

Carina pushed a wad of Play-Doh into Laurie's hands. Laurie rolled a small blue-and-red ball and handed it to her.

"Oh, sanks!" The little girl beamed at her, and promptly smashed the ball flat.

"Do it again, Laurie. Do it again!" she begged. So Laurie started another ball.

I watched my pregnant daughter. For the thousandth time a wave of sadness flowed over me. My first grandchild.

Yes, I could understand why the girl's family had chosen to ignore the situation. There was pain in walking through this experience as a family. But we'd been in hard places before, and God had been faithful. Each time we had faced our circumstances, acknowledged our failures, accepted forgiveness, and walked on, we had always come through the other side stronger and closer together. This time the pain was more intense, but we had consciously chosen to accept it. Trying to deny it could only drive it deep, to fester and grow, and reappear some other day.

Carina climbed onto what was left of Laurie's lap.

"Hug, Laurie!" she demanded, wrapping her little arms tightly around her older sister's neck. They had passed for mother and daughter more than once, with the same blonde hair, golden skin, and blue eyes.

"Thank You, Jesus," I breathed. "Thank You for the love between those two. Laurie needs that little girl right now, and pretty soon she may need her even more."

Already Laurie was getting a little preview of the emotional pain ahead of her. Just yesterday a friend's child had asked her when her baby would be born.

"Then will you bring it for me to see?" the child asked excitedly. Yes, there was pain.

"Oh, Mom," Laurie said suddenly, trying to disentangle herself from her little sister, "did I show you any of the notes and letters I got from people at school before I left there?"

"No, I guess not," I answered, pulling Carina loose.

Laurie got up slowly, one hand on the small of her back.

"Backache?" I asked.

"Oh, sort of." She frowned. "Something seems to have shifted in the last day or so. Everything seems lower—tighter."

"You look as if the baby has dropped," I observed, and then laughed. "When I was expecting Lynn, I went to visit the doctor at the end of October. He said the head was engaged and she could be born any time."

Laurie looked at me wide-eyed. "But Lynn was born at Christmas!" she exclaimed.

"I know." I laughed again. "Don't worry. Four weeks will go quickly. Now, get those letters."

Laurie went to her bunk, still holding her back. When she returned she handed me a card.

"This is from a girl at school who was adopted. I didn't know her very well, but she'd been watching me. She had felt bitter toward her natural mother. She couldn't believe that her mother had loved her, because she'd given her up for adoption."

The small note read,

My mamma once
Stood where you are now.
Somehow
In your eyes I see
Her love for me.
Your tears
Are those she cried
For my life

In her fear and hurting.
And
To see it now,
Somehow
Pulls back a curtain
Too long drawn closed.
Pain is revealed
And scars are healed
In the light
Of His love
In your eyes.

I was still recovering from the first note when she handed me the second.

Dear Laurie,

Thank you for staying in school and choosing to be vulnerable and honest. You have had a deep effect on my life by allowing me to watch yours, to see your fears and decisions.

Seeing you go through your pregnancy has brought forcefully to my mind and heart the very real consequences of the focusing of dating on the physical. It's caused me to very seriously seek God and be honest about even small areas that are not pleasing to Him in my dating.

Laurie, your making right choices and your humility that allowed God to make your pregnancy a time of growth and beauty have definitely affected those around you.

The fruit of obedience will be seen even years down the road. The impact of sin is great; but the impact of obedience is even greater.

Thank you, Laurie, for being tender-hearted and obedient.

The third letter was from a roommate.

> Dear Laurie,
>
> . . . I look back at the first time I talked to you
> . . . somehow I knew that there would be a special
> relationship between us . . .
>
> . . . He brought you to me for such specific
> purposes.
>
> Like the first time I really hurt and you decided
> it was about time you stopped getting comfort and
> started reaching to others' needs.
>
> So you were there, and it was the first of many
> beautiful talks that we've had about human behav-
> ior, God's will, and God's plan.
>
> And then when I found out you were preg-
> nant—oh, the pride I felt to have been chosen by
> God to share in this experience with you in such a
> close and specific way!
>
> I've been able to experience the very core of
> you as I've watched you struggle and endure with
> so much God-given grace and patience. He's taught
> you to deal with all sorts of characters in a very
> loving way.
>
> But, mostly, I've been a "guest of honor,"
> seated in the Artist's workshop as He patiently,
> gently, skillfully, and lovingly whittled away with
> a hammer, chisel, and sandpaper at what was once
> rough-hewn, and has now become a most beautiful
> sculpture which is yet daily taking on the likeness
> of Christ. I've always found art shows thrilling,
> and this one has simply and powerfully moved my
> heart. . . .
>
> What a delight for me to say, "This is Laurie,
> she's my roommate, and she's very special to me.
> I'm honored to know her and to be a part of her
> life."

When I finished reading, my eyes were wet. I was extremely grateful for the way God had used my daughter, proof positive that He could bring His good out of the most unlikely circumstances.

Rrrring!

"It's probably for you, Laurie."

It was. Sometimes the reception on the cordless wasn't very clear inside the bus, so Laurie went down the steps and out the door.

I watched her strolling on the freshly mown lawn. The fruit trees were in glorious blossom, pale pink, snowy white, full of the promise of life. Laurie fit the picture well with her blonde hair flowing in the sun and her round body full of the promise of life. She turned back toward the bus, smiling widely.

"You look happy," I said as she came back up the steps and put the phone down.

"I am *so* excited!" Laurie beamed. "That was the lady from the adoption agency. She just told me about a family for the baby, and they sound absolutely perfect."

She had been praying that the first family the agency came up with would be right, and she would know it. The lady who was working with Laurie had been considering this particular family for some time, but she hadn't said anything. Instead she and her co-workers prayed for wisdom. At the same time, the unknown family was also praying, and of course, we were all praying.

We had been warned that Laurie wouldn't want to hear anything about her baby's adoptive family. I was greatly relieved to see her joy in answered prayer.

"Laurie," I said, "you seem to have settled that 1 percent of doubt you had about giving the baby up. Is that true?"

She didn't answer right away. Her head dropped a little and she looked at me out of the corners of her eyes. There was a sheepish grin on her face. "Well, actually, I made my final decision the day I left school."

Startled, I said the first thing that came to my mind. "Why didn't you tell us?" But even as I spoke, I knew the answer to my question. The decision was a private one, and keeping it private for a while sealed it in her mind. In her situation I probably would have done the same thing. When she spoke, she confirmed my thoughts.

"I guess I needed time to adjust to it myself before I made a statement. I knew it would be reality once I actually said it."

"I understand," I assured her. "You just caught me off guard."

She looked thoughtful. "You know, I think I expected to have doubts about my decision. But the peace God gave me at that point has never left me. My emotions come and go, but that deep, inner peace is always there."

We talked into the afternoon. I noticed that Laurie was squirming and rubbing her back occasionally. She seemed to get more uncomfortable toward the end of each day.

We'd been so engrossed that neither of us had heard Tom and Dawn drive in.

The bus door opened and Tom poked his head in. "Hi. How are the rest of my girls?" he asked cheerily.

He and Dawn came in. Dawn knelt to hear Carina's excited account of her day. Tom hugged us, and poked Laurie's tummy gently.

"My, it's a hard little ball today." He grinned.

"Oh, I'm really tired of being pregnant, Daddy." She held her ankles up for him to see. "Look how puffy and swollen they are! I feel puffy all over. Sometimes I think I'll always be fat." She stuck her lower lip out just the way she had as a three-year-old.

That weekend Laurie finally had a chance to talk to our midwife friend, Signe. She and I practiced some breathing techniques. We promised to continue to practice them until we met with Signe again.

Signe was very encouraging. She told Laurie that she was in great condition and that she'd do just fine during labor. She also offered to be a backup coach if Laurie would like her to. Laurie very definitely would.

I was delighted, too. I wasn't all that confident in my own performance, even though we still had plenty of time to practice.

Laurie hadn't seen her official midwife since Christmas and was anxious to visit her again. We drove to town together. Laurie dropped me off to run some errands while she went to see Inger.

"Well, how did it go?" I asked when her visit was over.

Laurie wrinkled her nose at me. "You know how I love those check-ups." She squirmed in the seat. "Actually, I'm pretty uncomfortable. I think I feel like I'm in labor."

"Yeah, those examinations always make you feel that way," I said reassuringly. At the same time I eyed her suspiciously.

"Inger says the baby could come a little sooner than we thought."

"That would be a record in this family." I laughed. "But, you know, you may want to cancel your plans tonight and tomorrow—just in case." I tried to sound nonchalant.

"Oh, Mom, we're only going about seventy-five miles." She planned to spend the night nearby with Lynn and then travel with her to see cousins the next day.

Well, I was probably being silly. But that night I called Laurie at Lynn's to see how she was.

"I'm just fine," she laughed. "Relax, Mom."

When we went to bed, I made sure that the phone was nearby.

11
A CHILD IS BORN

R*rring!* I leaped over Tom and ran to the front of the bus. I glanced at the clock. 5:45 A.M.

"Laurie?" I knew she was the one calling.

"Mom?" She sounded scared. "I don't *want* to be in labor!" Then she started to cry.

"Calm down, sweetheart. Tell me what's happening."

Laurie sniffled awhile, then got hold of herself. "I slept in Lynn's bed last night—or anyway I tried. But I had this weird backache, and I just couldn't get comfortable. I kept thrashing around and waking Lynn up. In the middle of the night I started having contractions. They're sort of irregular, but I feel like I have cramps."

"What does 'irregular' mean?" I asked.

"Oh, they're five, eight minutes apart."

"Can you drive?"

"Sure. It doesn't hurt that bad. It's probably not even for real. I feel silly."

"Don't worry about feeling silly, sweetie. You come, and then we'll decide what's happening. I'll call Signe."

"What's going on?" Dawn poked her sleepy head around the corner.

"Laurie's probably having a baby," I answered on my way to the back of the bus.

Tom was wide awake. "Should she be driving?" he asked, worried.

"Oh, she's not far away—she's OK."

Calling Signe's house, I discovered that she'd been out since midnight, attending a birth. I dialed the number her husband gave me.

"Hello?" someone answered. There was a newborn's cry in the background. *Good!* I thought. *She's free.* Signe agreed to meet us.

Tom was still lying in bed when I got back there, but wide-eyed. I lay down beside him to wait for Laurie, the adrenaline ebbing a bit.

Laurie drove in beside the bus. The engine stopped. A minute or two passed without her coming in. Tom sat up and yanked back the curtain to look out.

"She's not moving!" he exclaimed.

"She's probably having a contraction, honey," I said, but he pulled on his pants and reached for a shirt.

Before he got to the front of the bus, Laurie came in. She looked a bit tired but pretty calm.

I hugged her. "Well, honey, maybe you're on your way! Just think. No more waiting."

She and I took seats as Tom fired up the big diesel engine. We picked up Signe and called Inger who said she'd meet us at the hospital.

On the way, Signe assured us that there was plenty of room in the hospital parking lot for our thirty-five-foot bus. Arriving at the gate, we explained our situation. Much to our amusement, they issued us a Commercial Delivery Pass, and we parked right next to the hospital. Lynn soon arrived and, of course, Carina was awake by then. When Inger got to the hospital, she joined us in the bus, where she examined Laurie and had some tea with us. She was surprised, but pleased, that Laurie could spend her labor "at home."

Two close friends of our family, Rhoda and Shaye, had heard where we were and couldn't resist joining us. Laurie was delighted to see them.

The day was peaceful as we fell into a routine that, of course, revolved around Laurie. People came and went, took turns walking Carina, recorded the time and duration of labor pains, and coached Laurie with her breathing. Rhoda and Shaye brought Laurie a very unique stuffed frog for her collection, along with a big chocolate egg they'd had to buy because Carina had taken the foil wrapper off of it in the store.

We drank tea, talked quietly, rubbed Laurie's back and feet, prayed with her, reassured her, timed her contractions.

During a lull between contractions, Rhoda brought Laurie a Bible. It was opened to 1 Samuel and the story of Hannah.

"This is for you, Laurie," Rhoda said softly, handing her the Bible. Laurie quietly read the story of Hannah's distress at her barrenness. When God had answered her prayer and given her a son, she had taken him to the temple and given him to God, literally. She said, "I have lent him to the Lord; as long as he lives he is lent to the Lord" (1 Samuel 1:28 RSV). Then Hannah prayed and rejoiced, worshiping God as she left her child in His hands and returned home (1 Samuel 1:19–28; 2:1–11).

God was continuing to prepare Laurie to do that same thing. She remained peaceful and calm.

At about 5:30 P.M., we walked Laurie to Shaye's car and drove her to the hospital door. She went the rest of the way to the birthing room in a wheelchair.

The room was as close to being "home" as we could have hoped for: brass bed with brown sheets, flowered wallpaper, and curtains. Laurie was propped up with a brown bean-bag chair!

As her labor became more intense, those of us who were coaching her were amazed at the way she followed orders. Inger said she was "elegant." We alternately laughed and cried, watching her work through each contraction.

"Hee-hee-hee-pah!" she breathed daintily, the picture of concentration. If there had been fear before, there certainly was none now. She had a job to do and she was going to do it right.

By the time she was well into the transition stage, there were thirteen close friends and family at hand. We were all exceedingly aware of God's presence there. In spite of the intensity of the moment, the room was pervaded with peace. The support and acceptance of everyone there was overwhelming. Occasionally I looked up at my family at the foot of the bed—Lynn, Dawn, and Tom holding Carina. The love in their faces was so obvious, as they practically experienced Laurie's contractions with her.

Laurie's composure slipped a little, and her "hee-hee-hee-pah's" began to come out "ha-hee-hoo-ha-ho-hee!" She sounded as if she had a big mouthful of hot oatmeal! But as soon as the pushing began, she really got down to business.

Inger held a mirror for Laurie so she could watch her own progress. It was hard work pushing the baby out, and she wanted to make sure she was really doing it. A couple of us held her head up, someone else propped her legs up, everyone told her to "Push, Laurie! Good girl! That was just great! You're doing fine!"

She got more and more determined as time went on. Inger had a little trouble holding the mirror just right, and sometimes Laurie couldn't see as well as she wanted to.

A big contraction came along and Inger said, "Up with the head, tuck in your chin, hold your breath, and *push!*"

Laurie, red face all scrunched up, chin in, growled through clenched teeth, "Can't *see!*"

We laughed, the mirror was righted, and work went on. A few minutes later in the middle of a big push, Laurie reached up with both feet, grabbed the mirror between them, and tilted it back into place. Everyone collapsed with laughter that time!

Then a gargantuan push, and there was a breathless hush as the baby's head appeared. Another push, and a little girl was born.

Such a mixture of joy and sorrow, tears and laughter I've never experienced. I remember bodies jumping up and down like pistons at the end of the bed. "You did it! You did it!" Everyone was smiling and crying and hugging, and Jesus was there!

The little girl weighed almost seven pounds. She was beautiful. Dark hair and dark, almond-shaped eyes in a pixie-like, pink face. She was petite and perfect.

I looked at Laurie through my tears. Her face was the picture of peace and strength. My memory of the next few minutes is rather hazy, but I remember Inger handing me a pair of surgical scissors and asking if I wanted to cut the cord. I took the scissors and placed them on the thick white-and-blue cord. I was surprised that it cut so easily. And there she was. On her own. Laurie's baby. My granddaughter.

I'll never understand how Jesus took our sorrow and transformed it so that the memories of that short time with the baby are not bitter but truly sweet. Sad, but sweet.

Inger wrapped the baby in a white, flannel blanket and handed her to Laurie. She pushed the blanket away from the little face and smiled at her, a beautiful smile.

"Hi," she said. When she had held her for about fifteen minutes, a nurse walked in.

"Oh! She should be holding the baby on her bare tummy. Let's warm that baby up."

I almost panicked. This bonding procedure wasn't supposed to happen. It would only make letting go harder for Laurie. My mouth opened, but before any words came out, I got a glimpse of Laurie's face. She was still smiling and peaceful. I gulped and watched as the baby was unwrapped and laid on Laurie, skin-to-skin.

I stood watching the two of them, knowing that these would be the only moments that they would share as mother and daughter. Laurie was smiling at her little girl, stroking her hair and cheeks, talking softly to her.

It was too much all of a sudden. I had to escape. This had happened too fast. The baby wasn't even supposed to be here yet!

The baby! She'd been born a month sooner than the date we'd given the adoption agency! That meant that the adoptive parents weren't alerted and the baby might be left at the hospital for who knows *how* long. I turned and hurried from the room, glad for a truly valid excuse.

I had a hard time getting my call through, but I finally succeeded. When I returned to the room, half an hour later, Laurie was still holding her baby. But Inger stood beside her with the white blanket. She gently lifted the baby from Laurie's arms and wrapped her up again. She picked up the tiny bundle and stood beside the bed.

Laurie suddenly asked to see the little fingers and toes. Inger unwrapped them and Laurie carefully inspected each hand and foot.

She wept a few tears when Inger walked away. Signe leaned toward Laurie and whispered in her ear, "Remember, she's the Lord's baby."

The peace had never left Laurie's countenance. I saw Inger's face, though, as she left the room, and I cried for her. Someone asked her later if she'd had to take a baby away like that very often. She said simply, "If I did, I'd hate my job."

Everyone but family and the two midwives soon left the room. Laurie spent the next three hours resting, talking quietly with Inger and Signe, eating, and waiting to be released from the hospital.

When the three hours were up, we took her back out to the bus, tucked her into bed, and drove out of the parking lot. Laurie was sound asleep before we'd gone a mile.

12
AFTERPAINS

The amazing peace that surrounded Laurie at the birth continued into the next day. She had slept soundly and woke refreshed.

"Mom! I slept on my stomach!" she exclaimed. Then her face clouded. "Speaking of my stomach, look at it. I still *look* pregnant!"

Signe checked Laurie and declared she was doing fine. She would be sore for a while from all the pushing, and when her milk came in, she'd be uncomfortable for a few days. But we were very thankful that everything was progressing normally.

Later in the day, Signe's five-year-old daughter, Carmen, came to see her mom. She wanted to say hello to Laurie, too.

"Where's your baby?" Carmen asked innocently.

Signe quietly explained, "You remember Jamie Adams? Well, Laurie gave her baby to a family just like his, a family who couldn't have children of their own."

I was sitting on Laurie's bed, watching her face. At first it registered nothing. Then suddenly there was such a pleading and pain-filled look in her eyes that my own brimmed with tears.

"Mom?" she called softly. "Oh, Mom, I feel so awful."

I knew she wasn't referring to how she felt physically. "Of course you do, honey."

"It's like she died."

I swallowed hard against tears. "It is, and it's OK to grieve. It's OK to cry. You've lost someone you loved."

"I did. I loved her. I still love her. I always will."

"All of us always will."

"I'm just glad I know I did what God wanted me to. I don't think I could stand it otherwise."

"Before the baby was born," Signe said, "I asked God about the wisdom of the adoption." She smiled and took Laurie's hand. "He assured me that I should support you in this decision. You have made a wise choice, a hard choice, a godly choice."

Her words comforted Laurie. Yes, we were experiencing sorrow, but it was a peaceful sorrow.

Tom, the girls, and I had been carried through the past hours, wrapped in love and prayer. We were free to laugh, cry, and react spontaneously. Everyone around us had suffered and rejoiced with us. I felt warmed and sustained, and God's presence had never seemed more real.

Into this insulated cocoon came the first jarring notes. I was totally unprepared.

We suddenly discovered that some of the people in our lives were struggling with anger and hurt. They couldn't understand how we could give away a child. There had even been prayer meetings, asking God to "save the baby."

My emotions were so frayed I couldn't sort out the motivations behind what was being said. I simply felt attacked and terribly hurt. I also felt betrayed, especially by God.

I cried out, "Lord, You've been so faithful to answer our questions and guide us. And now I feel misunderstood and mistreated. After all, isn't it enough that we have to deal with the pain of giving the baby up? Why should we have to work through feelings of rejection, too?"

For days I carried around the weight of that misunderstanding. I stopped leaning on God for the answers and started arguing with myself and having imaginary conversations in my head. I told those who disagreed with us quite clearly how wrong they were, something I would never do in real life.

All too soon the caseworker from the adoption agency brought the relinquishment papers for Laurie to sign. Tom, Laurie, and I sat down with the woman and talked for a while.

"I can tell you that the adoptive parents are thrilled with the baby," she said. "They are already totally in love with her."

"I'm so glad," Laurie said. "I've prayed for them, and I know they'll take good care of her for me."

I watched her face for some sign of panic—panic that I was suddenly feeling myself.

My stomach lurched as Laurie picked up the pen and began to write her name. I wanted to shout, "Stop!" It seemed too easy, giving away a human life by a mere signature. Accusing voices seemed to shout in my ears, "Save the baby!"

By the time the papers were signed, Laurie's expression told me she was feeling the finality of it all.

"Lord, help us!" I prayed desperately. I didn't dare look at Tom. I was afraid he'd mirror my feelings and say something about it.

The four of us sat and talked quietly for a few more minutes. We prayed together and cried a little. By the time the lady left, I was peaceful again.

Laurie sat staring straight ahead. Suddenly she wailed, "I want my baby!" and cried as though her heart would break. Tom and I held her, but there wasn't anything to say. My own heart felt beyond repair.

Later that night we sat on Laurie's bed with her.

"I do want my baby. But I'm also glad I don't have her. I know it would be wrong for her and wrong for me," she said. "That's one thing I'll always be sure of."

Right then I realized that Laurie hadn't doubted God for one moment. She had remained firm from the moment she made her decision. I also saw that other people's disapproval hadn't made her question that decision. She'd felt hurt, but she wasn't nearly as affected as I was by what people thought.

I was ashamed of myself. If anyone should be having second thoughts, it was Laurie. And here I was, falling apart at the seams!

In bed that night, I told Tom what I had been struggling with. He held me close and admitted some of the same feelings.

"I never expected it to be so hard," he said. "I wanted to bring that little girl home with us so badly."

Then I had another realization.

"Tom! You're a grandpa!" I couldn't help but giggle a little. It seemed so strange. "Grandma and Grandpa Lewis."

"We'll always be her grandma and grandpa," Tom whispered in my ear, "just like Laurie will always be her mother."

The next morning Laurie woke up swollen with milk. Milk for her baby who wasn't there to drink it.

Signe had been right. She was uncomfortable for a few days. But for the most part, she only complained about the physical discomfort.

Since Laurie couldn't wear normal clothes yet, she felt awfully fat.

"I never thought I'd wish to be flat-chested again!" she laughed wryly. "Between this and my saggy stomach I feel *huge*."

In the weeks that followed, we talked a lot as a family, and in twos and threes. A fresh closeness had come to us as we shared Laurie's life with her. There was a new awareness that God truly could be trusted with every imaginable circumstance, even in our feelings of being misunderstood.

Together, Laurie and I wrote a letter to the people who were upset with us. We didn't ask people to agree with Laurie's decision. We only asked them to trust God in our lives, even if they didn't understand.

I wrote half of the letter and Laurie wrote the other half. Toward the end she wrote,

> To say that I don't ever wish I could have kept her, or that I don't ever hurt, would be a lie. But there is a peacefulness inside like I never expected to have. We're all God's children. Just as you have put your own children in His hands, I've put my baby in His hands. Only in a more physical way . . .

Laurie continued to be the strong one in the situation, though she sensed a growing awkwardness in the presence of some people. More than once, she helped me to overlook the very human reactions. The fact that she was OK certainly helped.

One day I was thinking and praying about my feelings of being misunderstood and rejected. It occurred to me that if *we* were childless and adopting a baby, everyone would be thrilled to death. Would there be any thought for the natural mother then?

The Lord brought me up short with a startling interruption in my line of thought. It came, seemingly from nowhere, but I knew better.

The thought was, *If it had been someone else instead of you, would you be any more willing than your critics to face the pain of letting the baby go? Haven't you been just as prone to avoid pain and conflict in other situations?*

I humbly remembered how I had run from Tom's telephone call to Laurie. In fact, it seemed to me that the tendency to avoid pain at all costs was a characteristic of our society.

A close friend had recently had a miscarriage. She and her husband were going through a definite period of mourning for their lost child. In a letter to me she said,

> . . . I guess it's just hard to let ourselves feel the pain because it's not culturally acceptable. It's kind of an easy-come-easy-go world and when something really reaches your inner guts with pain, it's not popular to accept it. . . .

I knew the anguish that people were feeling about the giving up of the baby was real. But it was made so much more intense by lack of communication. They hadn't told us how they felt about adoption because they hadn't wanted to hurt us.

They hadn't let themselves become a part of our experience because they hadn't wanted to face the pain in it for themselves. And, again, because of lack of communication, they had no understanding of the process through which Laurie's decision had been made.

However, I had confidence in the overriding love in these relationships. I knew they might never agree with the decision that was made.

But I was quite sure they would respect the fact that the decision had been made in the honest belief that God was asking for that choice. And that was all that mattered.

It amazed me the way that God was working out His will in everyone. Laurie was able to express herself in more depth and with more ease than I'd ever dreamed would be possible. She and I spent many hours talking while Tom was at work and Dawn was in school.

"Don't you ever get tired of hearing me talk?" she asked me one day.

I laughed at her. "You can never talk too much for me, and don't you ever forget it."

"Well, our discussions have done wonders for me. You know, I've been forcing myself to keep things out in the open. If I feel sad, I cry. If I need to talk, whether I want to or not, I talk."

There were visible changes in Laurie. She was not the bouncing, carefree teenager she'd been the year before. Nor would she ever be that again. I felt a bit of a sense of loss as I watched her, but I knew that the changes were good.

There was a beauty and maturity developing in her that were rare in one of her age. The aura of sadness about her was not a harsh, bitter thing. It was somehow soft and gentle, mourning in a healthy sense. We all experienced that sadness on various levels. We didn't try to ignore or bury it. Instead we accepted the pain of our loss and continually asked for God's healing.

I kept wishing that Laurie would wake up some morning and everything would be all better, but that just didn't happen. She certainly didn't mope around and feel sorry for herself. She went out, participated in all of our family doings, got a job, bought a car, and proceeded with her life. She smiled a lot, but the sadness showed through.

One day as we stood in our bus, she casually told me, "I named my baby."

"You did?" I was startled. I knew she'd been looking at books of names before the baby was born. But when she was born early, I thought she'd abandoned that project.

"Well, what name did you pick?" I asked.

"Elise Joy," she smiled. "Elise means consecrated to God, and Joy is because of John 16:21."

I remembered how important that verse had been during Laurie's pregnancy and at the birth. ". . . She forgets the anguish because of her joy that a child is born into the world." I hugged my precious daughter, both for herself and for little Elise Joy.

Even though living in the bus had its drawbacks and we all got claustrophobia at times, I could see God's wisdom in allowing us to be so physically close through Laurie's weeks of recovery.

One Saturday about a month after the birth there was a big picnic on the lawn beside the bus. About fifty friends and family were there. We had sack races, wheelbarrow races, stunts, and a barbeque.

Laurie sat on the sidelines, still a bit sore from her delivery. Some of the children kept begging her to come and play. They were used to seeing her very active. I could tell that her sense of humor was getting strained with their teasing.

Also at the picnic was a young couple with their first child. The baby was only about a week older than Laurie's little girl. Laurie sat with them and even held the baby.

She appeared to be fine, but I kept an eye on her. When she disappeared, I went looking for her. She was in the bus combing her hair.

"I'm going for a walk," she announced airily. She put down her comb, squeezed toothpaste on her toothbrush, and started brushing vigorously.

Something didn't seem right. We hadn't really talked much all week. Something about the way she was brushing her teeth prompted me to ask, "Is anything bothering you, honey?"

The brushing stopped and Laurie stood up, her mouth full of white, minty foam. She started to cry. I don't remember what happened to that toothpaste, but she must have spit it out!

I held her and let her cry, sensing that something deep was going on inside of her. After she'd quieted a little, I asked, "Would you like me to get some others to come and pray with you?"

She immediately said, "Yes!"

I asked who she wanted and she specified Tom, Rhoda, and Signe.

We all sat with her on Tom's and my bed in the back of the bus.
We held her hands and listened to her. She poured out the hurt
and tension that had grown during the afternoon. Then she shared
something else that had been building inside of her.

"All week I've been fighting bitter feelings toward Rick. At first I
tried to ignore them, but it keeps getting worse. I feel angry that he's
gotten off so easy, and I had to go through nine months of pregnancy.
Then I was the one who had to make all the decisions and feel all the
loss. It doesn't seem fair!" She started crying again.

We cried with her and prayed for her. It became very clear that
the surgery on her soul was continuing. In order for the wounds to
be healed, they had to be opened and cleansed. She had to name the
injustice on Rick's part, in order to forgive him. That process hurt. It
was painful to face the facts, or even think about them again. How I
prayed that we would be patient and sensitive to her need during the
healing process, however long it took.

13
WITH HEALING IN HIS WINGS

I could almost *see* the healing that was happening in Laurie as she was willing to voice her honest thoughts and feelings.

One night, Tom and I had just gotten in bed when Laurie came home from a meeting she'd attended with friends. She crept in to see if we were awake.

"Hi, Laurie!" Tom greeted her. "Was it a good time?"

"The most wonderful thing happened to me," Laurie answered. Her voice was awed. "We were singing and worshiping, and my eyes were closed. We sang about the Lord being a shield about us, about Him being our glory and the lifter of our heads.

"All of a sudden it was like I was back in that birthing room. I saw myself exactly as I had been in the last stages of labor. I was bearing down, pushing with all my might, at the very peak of a contraction.

"Then I saw Jesus. He was sitting behind me, holding my head up. The lifter of my head!

"The scene changed and I saw myself sitting there, holding my baby. Jesus stood beside the bed. I was aware of a deep peacefulness flowing around the three of us.

"I knew Jesus was waiting for me to hand Him the baby, but He wasn't in a hurry. When I finally put my baby into His arms, He took her gently. He stood there holding her so that I could see her. He looked lovingly at the baby, then at me, and back at the baby. He never did walk away."

We were speechless except to whisper, "Thank You, Jesus."

Then there was the letter from the adoptive mother. She had sent it to Laurie through the adoption agency along with a picture of the baby, taken shortly after birth.

To our dear sister in Christ,

There isn't a day goes by that we don't think of you and pray for God's peace to dwell in your heart . . . and yet, when it came to actually writing our thoughts down in this letter, I, at least, have suffered great uncertainty about how to express our true feelings in a way that would bring comfort and peace of mind—not worry or regret. You have given us the greatest gift we've ever received from anyone and yet we do not know you. Surely you have wondered sometimes where your step in faith has taken the child you bore. I cannot write this without crying—we love her so much, we are so thankful, we are so humbled by the awesome privilege of raising her. And always we are aware of you, your family, and the difficult decision you were faced with. We realize now that when we say "our" child she is *all* of ours—for, as we are one in Christ, so we are one with each other. She is in you and you are in her. We cannot forget this and it makes our parenting task that much more precious. Thank you for trusting God so much that you could give us this most longed for opportunity . . .

She went on to tell Laurie many details of their home life and of their fascination with their new daughter. There was a loving description of her development and characteristics. She said,

> She is a beautiful child, and the delight of our lives . . .
>
> As I close this letter, I am reminded of Jesus' words from the cross to Mary and His beloved disciple: "Dear woman, here is your son," and to the disciple, "Here is your mother." He really understands adoption—its anguish and pain, its tenderness and joy. We give you our deepest love and respect.
>
> Your sister and brother in Christ

Along with and in between the times of healing were periods when we'd all get so busy with our day-to-day lives that we ignored our feelings for a while.

One night, after such a time, I found myself acknowledging intense pain. I got alone to write in my journal and communicate with the Lord.

> Please comfort Laurie tonight. She is really feeling the loss of her baby right now and doesn't want to admit it, even to herself.
>
> She cried tonight while I held her. Me, too, Lord. I've been doing the same thing she has. "I don't have time to cry right now," or "It's not convenient. Therefore it doesn't really bother me." Then, of course, there was always the thought, "God is healing me, so I don't want anybody to know I still hurt sometimes."
>
> Laurie has pain because she aches to hold that little girl of hers—to love her, care for her. I have pain both for Laurie and me, because I have a little granddaughter I'll never know.

I know what Laurie means when she says she doesn't know what to do with the pain when it comes. I don't either. I guess I feel like she needs so much more healing than I do that I shouldn't waste tears on myself. But trying to ignore it doesn't help.

Please teach us about sorrow. Help us not to miss the blessing You have for us in this pain. Help us to yield to You in it.

Fill the vacuum in all of us, especially in Laurie. Heal her, please. And heal the ache in my heart, too. I know I haven't lost anything. Not really. I'll know my granddaughter in heaven, and she'll always be my first grandchild.

But I can't just say things like that and have them wipe the pain away. Thank You that the aching sends me into Your arms. Many times I avoid that place because there my hurts are exposed and I have to face them.

Time. It *was* taking time, and much more than we had thought. Yet every step brought us closer to wholeness. Each sore place that was opened up received more of the balm of God's healing.

One day Laurie was feeling particularly down about the way her body looked. She stood peering at herself in a full-length mirror, scowling. Her tummy wasn't quite flat yet, and she'd put on a few pounds. She looked great to me, but that didn't count for much.

"You know how I feel?" she asked suddenly, glaring at me. "I feel like Rick got it all. He took everything from me. My future husband will only get the leftovers." She bit her trembling lower lip, and a tear slid down her cheek. "It's not fair!"

Hmm—resentment. Very natural, but . . . "Laurie, tell me about Rick. You weren't doing much talking when you were involved with him."

She looked startled but wiped her eyes on her shirttail and plopped down on a bed.

"I didn't dare talk much," she admitted. "Didn't want anybody to interfere with my big fling before Bible school."

"When did you decide on that 'fling'? And why?" I asked.

Laurie almost smiled. "I think I was mad at God. Remember when I was visiting churches, trying to find one where I could get some encouragement? Find some friends?"

Yes, I remembered. Most of the people involved in our fellowship were either older or younger than our girls. We'd encouraged them to go out looking. But they had been "spoiled" by the close, personal relationships they had observed and been a part of for years.

"One day Lynn was away and I had to go to church alone," Laurie continued. "I went to a great big church that somebody had recommended. Nobody seemed to know I was even alive. The service was so cold and impersonal, and the pastor was trying to talk people into joining his church.

"All of a sudden I'd had it. Something snapped in my attitude. I walked out in the middle of the service and went to Rick's house."

"What were you thinking at that point?" I asked.

"Well, Rick didn't share my beliefs, but at least he knew I was alive. He seemed to fill needs in me that the churches I'd visited didn't."

"Did you feel like you were turning your back on God and choosing Rick's way of life?"

"No, not really, although God did seem pretty remote. And I really did want to get to know Rick, communicate with him." Laurie glanced at me out of the corner of her eye.

"I take it the communication didn't go all that well."

"Hah!" She curled up against the bed pillows. "We were never able to communicate beyond a few superficial things. I was scared that if I told him what I really wanted from our relationship, I'd lose him." She sighed. "He was older, wiser."

"You mean you felt you had nothing of any value to contribute to the relationship?"

"Well, yes and no," Laurie said slowly. "We went to a lot of neat places together, and I knew I was fun to be with. But then when we were quiet, we'd run out of things to say. We both got restless. Had to have something to do.

"So . . . we started kissing. After that, things progressed really fast. It seemed like the only way we could communicate was physically. Inside, I didn't want what was happening, but I didn't know how to get out of it."

She turned to look me in the eye. "I guess I didn't really want to get out of it badly enough, did I?" She smiled weakly. "It's crazy. I was crazy. I couldn't fully enjoy it because I had so much guilt and anxiety. Plus, I was scared of getting pregnant."

We sat in silence for a few minutes.

"Mom, I felt pretty abnormal. I just couldn't respond to him the way I thought I should be able to. That made me feel awfully insecure about myself sexually. You know—one more thing I'm no good at. I kept thinking, *Why do we spend so much time doing this when I know it isn't right?*"

She looked so miserable and ashamed. I reached out and took her hand.

"Laurie, women are funny creatures. About 99 percent of our sexual response is in our heads. There's no way you could give yourself permission to respond fully or enjoy what was happening given who you are and how you were raised."

I squeezed her hand and continued. "Your brain was full of fear and guilt and tension. There wasn't any possibility for you to be relaxed or peaceful. Besides, a woman needs to be able to really trust a man before she can be willingly vulnerable. Without that, there isn't much enjoyment. With it, there can be great delight."

Her eyes lit up. "So, I'm normal, huh?"

"Of course you are! Just thank God for your built-in conscience and inhibitions." I pulled her to her feet, turning her toward the mirror again. "And you're not 'all used up.' You're beautiful, inside and out."

"But, Mom," she wailed, "I eat too much! I know I'm using food for comfort, but sometimes I don't care enough to stop. Everybody says I'm skinny, but I don't like the way I look. It would be easier if I were fat. Then people wouldn't argue with me."

Using food for comfort. Yes, I understood that. Laurie and I seemed to be put together in a similar fashion. If I was extremely upset, I couldn't eat. But a little anxiety, a little frustration, and I became preoccupied with food.

Both of us loved the kitchen, loved to cook, and loved to eat. Like Laurie said, nobody would ever call either of us overweight, but we both knew the weight at which we felt best.

"Are you lonely, Laurie?" The thought seemed out of place. Where had that come from?

She had her back to me. There was silence for a few seconds and then I heard a little "Yes."

She didn't elaborate. She didn't have to. In circumstances that were less than ideal, Laurie had experienced some of the closeness God intended for marriage. She also had given birth to a child, and her mother-heart was awakened. Add to that the fact that she was a real home-body who loved to do all the domestic things involved in running a household. But there was no husband, no children, no home.

As if she had read my thoughts, she said, "I'm lonely, but at the same time I'm thankful I don't have anyone in my life right now. Not a husband, not a child."

"Really?"

"If I weren't lonely, I probably wouldn't take the time to pay attention to my hurts and wounds. Or the problems in my life either. I'd just ignore them all and go on with life."

"That's a very wise insight, honey."

She stood a bit straighter. "I'm learning so much! I get sick and tired of being sick and tired, but at times when I can see clearly, I understand what is happening. And this season won't last forever."

Then came the day when the adoptive parents sent Laurie a picture of her baby. We'd been expecting it, taken at six months.

Laurie wasn't home when the 5x7 brown envelope arrived. I could barely resist opening it. When she finally came home, she went off by herself with the envelope. When I found her later, I could tell she'd been crying hard.

"May I see it?" I desperately wanted to know what my granddaughter looked like. At the same time, I was afraid. Of what? My own emotion, I guess.

"I know she'll look very different from the way she was when she was born," I told myself. "I have to get prepared!" I clearly remembered the dainty pink-and-white bundle at the hospital. Dark hair, dark eyes peering at me.

Laurie handed me the envelope and I slid the picture out. *Wham!* My eyes immediately flooded with tears. I could barely see through the blur, but I'll never forget that first glimpse. She was a beautiful, alert, happy child. Big blue eyes, fair skin, a fringe of blonde hair, a smiling, rosy mouth. She looked very much the way Laurie had at that age.

The picture went into a frame in Laurie's bedroom, and it became one of her most prized possessions. At Christmas she had a 3x5 made and framed for Tom and me, and gave wallet-sized pictures to all of us. Tom's copy immediately went into his wallet, as a reminder to him to pray for his first grandchild.

Elise Joy, our granddaughter. Laurie's daughter. Her picture was a constant reminder of the beauty that God created, the loveliness He fashioned out of sorrow and pain.

The adoption agency strongly encouraged Laurie to write a letter to her baby. It was to be sent to the adoptive parents and given to Elise Joy when she was eighteen years old. At that time, both she and Laurie would decide whether or not they would meet.

Laurie had started that letter right after the birth. She gave her daughter all kinds of information about our family and the traits, talents, and gifts she might inherit. She told her why she had chosen to give her up, and how much she loved her.

As the weeks and months passed, the letter never seemed to quite get finished. I was a little concerned, because I knew the adoptive parents would be eager to read it. Some of the information would be very helpful to them in raising Elise Joy.

Finally, I decided to ask Laurie about it, not to nag, just to inquire.

At first, she didn't respond; then, "I've thought a lot about it. At first I really thought it was taking so long because I wanted it to say just what I meant. Then I think of something to add, something I want her to know. But there's more to it than that."

She looked at me tearfully and managed, "I don't really want to finish that letter. It's like finally saying good-bye. I just can't do it yet."

I couldn't see any reason to push her. There weren't any vital medical facts the baby's new parents needed to know immediately about either side of her family. Laurie would send the letter when she was ready.

One day I was casually looking through the mail that had just arrived. In one magazine was an article by an adoptive father. I hadn't read much more than the first paragraph when a sudden realization jolted me. This man was Elise Joy's adoptive father. Excitedly, I read on.

He was describing the pain, particularly for his wife, in not being able to have a child of their own. For a number of years he had ignored his own feelings, and his wife had been somewhat alone in her hurt.

But then, unexpectedly, as he glanced at a book written by parents who had lost a child, something happened:

> . . . As if from nowhere, right then, pain suddenly stabbed deep, pain of hunger and longing. Tears started to fill my eyes. The nerve, so long insulated by thick tissues of rationality, and perhaps disinterest, had finally been struck. I think you've suspected, my dear wife, that it just wasn't there—some male psychological quirk—but it was.
>
> From somewhere I could see him. Our child. Our someday maybe child. With his hand in mine, walking together, pals, down a wet country road in autumn. Stopping often to look at slugs and jewel-studded spider webs, lacey veins of half-rotted leaves and minute mushrooms. Damp air and smells and wet grass—and a small, warm hand. Continuity. The passing on of life. The potential. Lord, there's a lot of love stored up inside me, waiting to be given to a child, waiting to be shared with my wife.

Laughter and sorrow, hopes and dreams longing to be fulfilled. I know the ache now, too. But I didn't think it, I felt it and it hurt.

Today I still feel sad about not being able to have biological children, not being able to experience pregnancy and birth with my wife. But I can still be a parent without experiencing that, and I want to be. I want to love and be loved by a child, to participate in the miracle of a new life, to share a child's world and to be a family. Perhaps my overriding reason, though, is that I like kids. I like to play with them, to roughhouse and laugh with them. I just want to be a dad.

As a parent, I would like to provide a home for children in which they are free to grow up to be most fully and completely themselves. I would want them to know above all, that my love for them is unconditional, that I respect them for who they are, and that I will do everything I can to help them lead fulfilled lives. I believe that discipline is important, life is structured, there are do's and don'ts, and that they, as individuals, have responsibilities. But discipline must be in the context of love and understanding, and I don't want to stifle their freedom to simply be children. I guess finding the middle ground in all this is exactly what parenthood is all about.

My life goals and hopes for the future have changed. I used to dream about the ideal job, the ideal home, and things I wanted to accomplish in my life. Much of that was striving to be a great person in the eyes of others. Although I haven't forgotten these things, I know that they are no longer important. Slowly, God is teaching me to trust Him.

My goals right now are to live more simply, to share in loving, caring fellowship with others, to

> deepen my relationship with my wife, and to learn
> to love her better, to offer hospitality more unself-
> ishly, to live more fully in the present tense, and to
> grow closer to God. And one very important hope
> for the future is to have children in our home.

There was no doubt in my mind that the anonymous author was "our" adoptive father. A caseworker had shared a few lines of this very same testimony with Laurie when she'd been pregnant. Looking up, I watched Laurie peacefully reading across the room. Should I show her? I knew I had to.

I handed her the article. "Does this sound familiar?" I asked quietly. I sat down with her.

As she read, her cheeks flushed. "That's him! Oh, Mom, that's my baby's new father!"

Laurie finished the article, then went into the bathroom. I waited a few minutes and then followed her. She was crying.

"It's so beautiful," she sobbed. "It was wonderful to hear from the mother. But it just completes things to hear from the father. I needed to see what a great person he is."

Bittersweet. Many times that word continued to describe situation after situation. How welcome and refreshing was the sweetness, made even more precious by the accompanying pain.

14
THE GREAT LIE

"If I've ever found a cause worth climbing onto a soap box for, it would be this one," Tom declared fervently.

He'd been reading some material I'd given him concerning abortion. Laurie and I were in the middle of taking eighteen hours of intensive training, which was required for people who wanted to work with a crisis pregnancy center in our city.

The center offered free pregnancy tests and counselors for women to talk to confidentially. While the test was being run, each woman was shown films, one to educate her concerning the growth of a fetus and another to detail abortion methods.

She was then counseled compassionately and offered whatever assistance she might need to allow her to carry her baby to term. If she needed a place to live, an approved family would take her in. Anything else she needed, whether she gave her baby up for adoption or kept it, was offered to her. Maternity clothes, baby clothes, baby furniture, continued counsel and friendship. She was given a workable option to abortion.

As the week of training progressed, I thought back to my own pregnancy with Carina. Because I was forty, doctors were very surprised that I planned to carry my baby to term. One doctor was quite agitated.

"Don't you understand the risk you are taking, having a baby at your age?" he demanded. "Chances are high that you'll have a Downs syndrome child. Then you'll be a real burden on the state systems. They'll have to support your child in an institution, and think of the anguish for you and your family!"

I was almost five months along when I saw that doctor. He was extremely insistent that I "have an amniocentesis test immediately. That way, if your baby is defective, you can still abort it legally." Maybe the third-trimester abortion clinics weren't open yet.

He didn't tell me about the risks involved in amniocentesis— everything from infection to actually piercing the baby. He also didn't tell me that the test had originally been a last resort for women who had previously borne Downs syndrome babies and were insisting upon abortions. It was designed to prevent the abortion of healthy babies.

When I went home and repeated all the dire predictions and horror stories to my family, they were indignant. "We don't care if the baby is abnormal. It's our baby," the girls responded vehemently.

Tom just smiled at me. I already knew how excited he was about our little "surprise." And me? I never could have considered an abortion anyway.

Now, as I thought back over the experience, I suddenly realized how important that incident had been for Laurie. At the time, none of us had any idea that she would have to deal with the issue of abortion herself a couple of years later. But God knew. And He had allowed her to absorb the thinking and values that He had instilled in us. How thankful I was.

It wasn't always easy sitting in the training sessions. I wondered how Laurie would handle it all so soon after her baby's birth, but her compassion for others kept her going back time after time to listen intently to every word.

I began to see more and more what a courageous thing Laurie had done in carrying her baby to term. Any girl who made that hard choice should be applauded and honored. Instead, girls who chose life were forced to justify their decisions to give birth to their children.

It is so easy, so logical in our brainwashed society, to take the "simple" way out and get an abortion. No hassle. No problems. No regrets. No life-altering little one.

The problem is that nobody ever tells about the methods or risks in these operations. Nor do we hear from the women who have gone this route. They don't get to speak of feeling unsettled or restless, of experiencing guilt and remorse. Those who totally harden themselves or live in denial seem to find temporary release, but only those who are able to receive God's love and forgiveness ever become completely free from the guilt and anxiety.

I thought of the millions of women who had ignorantly and trustingly allowed their unborn children to be torn from their wombs. I wondered how many of them could possibly have gone through with their abortions if they had known just a few facts.

Personally, I had been amazingly ignorant concerning abortion until Laurie's experience had stirred my interest and curiosity. The more I learned, the more astounded I was at my ignorance.

I found myself wishing that each woman planning an abortion was required to receive a complete explanation of all the methods and risks involved. Then she would listen to her baby's vigorously beating heart (as early as three weeks). A third requirement might be that she watch a sonogram of her baby moving around inside of her. After this simple education, there would be no way that she could any longer believe the lie, "Oh, we are just going to remove a little tissue."

We learned that a ten-week-old fetus was essentially no different than one of twenty or even thirty weeks. More and more, medical science is discovering fascinating facts about the unborn baby and how even at four weeks all the body organs are functioning. There is amazing surgery being performed on babies in the womb to correct problems that would be devastating if left until birth.

One small booklet that we received in our training had a tremendous impact on me. It was titled *Abortion in America* and it was written by C. Everett Koop, M.D. and Gary Bergel.

I forced myself to read the simple facts I'd ignored for so long. One page briefly listed the five methods of abortion used currently in the United States.[2]

---

[2] See description of abortion methods in the appendix of this book.

On another page was a large picture of a hand holding an embryo sac in which was a tiny human, six to eight weeks old. Accompanying the picture was this story, told by a New York doctor, Paul Rockwell, M.D.:

> Eleven years ago while giving an anesthetic for a ruptured tubal pregnancy (at two months), I was handed what I believed to be the smallest human being ever seen. The embryo sac was intact and transparent. Within the sac was a tiny (one-third-inch) human male swimming vigorously in the amniotic fluid, while attached to the wall by the umbilical cord. This tiny human was perfectly developed, with long, tapering fingers, feet and toes. It was almost transparent, as regards the skin, and the delicate arteries and veins were prominent to the ends of the fingers. The baby was extremely alive and did not look at all like the photos and drawings of "embryos" which I have seen. When the sac was opened, the tiny human immediately lost its life and took on the appearance of what is accepted as the appearance of an embryo at this state (blunt extremities, etc.).

In the emotion of hearing stories like this, it was easy to get my focus so much on the threatened babies that I gave too little thought to the other victims, the mothers. What tremendous pressure "a little education" about abortion would bring to bear on an already severely pressured woman! Every situation is different, and some women (even married women) just don't want to be bothered with the responsibility of a child. But probably most unwanted pregnancies are unwanted for very understandable reasons.

Take, for instance, the daughter of a friend, fifteen-year-old Donna. The father is seventeen. He told her that if she loved him she would simply go and get an abortion. Her parents are divorced, and Donna is living with her mother. Her mother has had two abortions herself and told Donna she would be glad to pay for Donna's. Her father just said, "Get rid of it."

Donna confided in a friend who told her all the facts about abortion and the growing child inside of her. Donna learned how precious life is in God's sight, and decided that she could not go through with an abortion.

When she told her mother about her decision, her mother was extremely angry and informed Donna that she couldn't stay at home if she refused to end her pregnancy. She also told her that if she kept the baby after it was born, it wouldn't be welcome in her home. Donna's boyfriend and her father renewed their attempts to persuade her to have an abortion. There were tears, shouts of anger, fear, panic.

Donna found that she was actually angry at her friend for enlightening her. She could have gone ahead with an abortion in ignorance. But now she was trapped, seemingly with nowhere to turn.

In Donna's case, as in many others, there is a desperate need for people to help. Our training emphasized the fact that if we are going to indignantly cry out against abortion, then we had better be ready to shoulder the burden that these women will find unbearable.

Many women will need a place to live, a family to lean on during their pregnancy. Some who decide to raise their babies need help to get established even after their pregnancies. Girls like Donna need to be made aware of adoption as a possibility. Above all, these courageous women who refuse to take the easy way out need our love.

There are growing numbers of agencies that specialize in steering women with crisis pregnancies to the right places to receive the help they need. But they can't do the job without the rest of us. They are mostly staffed by trained volunteers, and they need supplies and willing homes for the women who come to them.

As our training continued, I thought again about how difficult it would have been for Laurie to try to forgive herself if she had decided to have an abortion. The pro-life movement made information and the facts readily available. Eventually, Laurie would have learned the whole truth.

I thought of things in my own past that I desperately wished could be erased, or at least that the memory could be gone. God's forgiveness wasn't the problem. It was complete for Laurie, for me, as well as for every woman who has had an abortion. The hard part lies in receiving that forgiveness. In forgiving oneself.

Yes, I was extremely grateful all the way around that Laurie had chosen to "tough it out." I knew God would continue to grant the strength she needed.

15
TURNING POINTS

Both Laurie and I grew very tired, physically and emotionally, as we worked our way through the Crisis Pregnancy Center training. But we were also fascinated by what we were learning.

I kept a watchful, protective eye on Laurie all week, but she appeared to be handling everything well—until the very last session.

The discussion was totally focused on adoption, foster care, how to work with girls who were giving up their babies, and their feelings in the whole process. The afternoon was to involve everyone in role-playing, portraying pregnant girls and counselors.

At the break I said, "Come on, Laurie. Let's go talk to the speaker. This will be our last chance." Laurie followed me to the front of the auditorium.

When our turn came, I encouraged her to share her own experience with him, which she did. She seemed a little nervous but communicated well.

On our way to the back of the auditorium, she broke down and began to cry. Surprised, I steered her to the foyer and out the door. Outside, she cried for a while, then got control of herself. We went back in and sat down. But a few minutes into the session, she leaned over and whispered, "I can't sit here."

"Let's go home," I suggested, and we got up and left.

In the car Laurie told me, "It was just too close to home. I've done fine all week, but it got to me this time."

It was now almost a year since Elise Joy had come into the world. As healing happened in Laurie, and I saw her eagerness to reach out to others, sometimes I forgot to watch for signs of "overload." I could inadvertently push her ahead of God in the process. Gradually, I learned that she would have to set her own pace.

One day I received a call from the adoption agency.

"We were wondering if you'd talk to Laurie about something," the caseworker began a bit hesitantly. "We are planning to put together a slide presentation on adoption to show in area churches and high schools. We feel that adoption is rarely, if ever, presented as an option to mothers of unplanned pregnancies. Do you think Laurie would be willing to come in, be interviewed, taped, and photographed?"

"Well," I said slowly, "I can't promise anything, but I'll certainly talk to her."

Later, I carefully approached Laurie on the subject.

"I'd love to!" she exclaimed, without a moment's hesitation. She called the caseworker back immediately.

The taping and photographing session lasted about four hours. There were two pregnant girls, Laurie, and another girl who had already had their babies. Also included were two adoptive mothers as well as adoption caseworkers.

"How did it go?" I asked Laurie when she came home.

"It was really good even though I was so nervous at first! It was that same old fear that always ties my tongue in knots. I feel like I have nothing worthwhile to say." Then she grinned. "It got better though. And by the time we were finished, I didn't want to quit!"

Several weeks later I received another invitation. There was a new radio station in our city. Tom, Laurie, and I were asked to share our story on a talk show that was designed to confront the real, nitty-gritty situations of life.

Again, Laurie agreed immediately, but the night before the program, Tom was admitted to the hospital because of an irregular, erratic heartbeat. He'd had problems with this off and on since his open-heart surgery. As a result Laurie and I arrived alone at the radio station. We were totally unrehearsed, having prayed that God would give us all that He wanted us to share.

"OK," we were told, "we need a teaser for the opening of the show. Let's just tape a short blurb from each of you."

Laurie's eyes got wide as we sat down in front of the microphones.

"Don't let her panic, Lord," I prayed.

With some help from the station people, we each wrote down a brief statement and got it taped in time for the broadcast. Then all of us prayed together that our time on the air would be pleasing to God and even be fun.

At one point, Laurie was asked, "Could you trace the significance of the process you went through? Just give us a taste of what was happening to you."

"OK," she hesitated, not really sure what was being asked. She began to tell about her first days at Bible school.

"After I'd been there for about three weeks, I went in for a pregnancy test. I found out I was pregnant, but . . ."

Her voice trailed off into silence, and she looked at me pleadingly.

Oh, no, I thought. Every time in the past that this panicked expression appeared in a public situation, she totally lost it. I feared the next thing would be tears, then more tears, and our radio interview would be all over.

The interviewer and I covered for her, and he said something about how difficult it was to discuss such a sensitive subject.

I looked at Laurie, expecting to see tears. Instead she was smiling! Confidently and clearly, she answered all the other questions she was asked, giving an honest testimony of the way that God had brought her through the pregnancy and birth.

Tom even got in on the interview by telephone from his hospital bed. He was asked how he had felt when he heard that Laurie was pregnant.

"Oh, it was something like getting thrown up against a brick wall, then you settle back down onto the floor—relax a little—find yourself in a state of numbness."

He went on to describe guilt feelings and subsequently the realization of God's forgiveness and the understanding that the next months would be "one step at a time."

The hour passed quickly, and we were actually sorry when it ended.

Later, I asked Laurie, "What happened in there? I thought you were going to fall apart!"

"I almost did! But then I told myself, 'No! You don't have to go to pieces. God is with you, just like He was all those other times you didn't know about.' So I sat up and smiled and enjoyed myself."

I hugged her, "That's wonderful. You are really getting a complete overhaul, aren't you?"

It was true. And the healing process included all of us, not just Laurie. Tom and I shared one of those painful-step-forward times with Laurie after she had spent several hours specifically praying about her growing-up years.

The three of us sat together. I held one of Laurie's hands, and Tom held the other as she struggled to tell us how she felt.

"There were times when I needed you and you weren't there," she said. "Like the time when all those other kids were living with us a few years ago. I know that God sent them to our home, and I loved them, too. But sometimes I felt like they were more important than I was."

Basically, there had been times when she had needed our attention, but she hadn't asked for it because other people "had bigger problems" or "needed us more." And to our regret we'd been too involved to notice.

"You know," Tom confessed openly, "I was always sort of embarrassed to play with you girls the way I did when no one was around." He grinned sheepishly. "Now I understand that this sort of relationship was exactly what the others needed to see."

Laurie squeezed his hand.

I helplessly remembered periods of time when I was terribly involved with other kids' drug problems or emotional upsets.

It wasn't that Tom and I ignored our kids. Their physical needs were always taken care of, and we planned special times with them.

Tom scheduled each daughter for a regular meal out. We were proud of our children and had good communication with them.

But apparently we hadn't been sensitive enough to them, hadn't "pried" enough.

So, I thought, tears running down my face, *that nagging doubt was a reality.* I couldn't deny it anymore. We really *had* blown it. The thing that I'd always hated to see in other parents—putting others before their own family—was the very thing we'd been guilty of.

Laurie forgave us quickly and easily because of the work God had been doing in her. She'd been very reluctant to tell us because she hadn't wanted to hurt us.

Tom had already come to grips with his failure in this area, but I found it hard to forgive myself. In the next couple of days I had some hot words with the Lord.

"What a dirty trick You played on us!" I accused Him. I never had and never would question the fact that God had sent all those young people to us. But now I was seriously questioning His wisdom.

"You knew all this would happen, and Lynn and Dawn probably have the same kinds of hurts. Why did You do it?"

As I gradually wound down, I was able to hear God's voice speaking to my heart. Little by little I gained understanding and peace as He showed me some facts.

1. God had, indeed, given us our ministry with young people.
2. We hadn't responded in a 100 percent correct manner, but we hadn't totally failed either.
3. We definitely made mistakes in raising our children. There still were no perfect parents.

My understanding grew in the form of a question and answer: What kind of people would we be if all those kids *hadn't* come into our lives?

I already knew the answer to that. Our life as a family had been headed in a deadly direction. We'd recognized the death in it and prayed for a change. In answer, God had filled our house.

I remembered how fearful, selfish, and exclusive Tom and I had been. We hadn't known how to communicate or be honest even with each other, let alone with anyone else.

God had taught us to love and give, and to let our lives be open books through those He'd sent. Our children had grown up without the terrible, competitive spirit their parents had to discard. They had watched the reality of God's promises and provision in very practical ways. And the list went on and on.

It didn't take long for me to be able to thank Him again for that part of our life. Sure, we'd made some serious mistakes. But I was grateful for the mistakes we'd been able to avoid.

And more than anything, I was very thankful to the Lord for the present. The love and understanding that He was building into our family was a priceless treasure. I saw that the key was in being repentant, forgiven, thankfully joyful, and going on from there.

Mother's Day came along soon after we had our talk with Laurie. She gave me a card with a picture of a funny little kid on it. The caption read: "I never tell people you're my mother! It might make them expect more of me!"

She had written a message inside:

Hi, Mom,

It's hard to believe a year has gone by since last Mother's Day. My, how we've changed, grown up, grown together. I feel like this last year has been one of the most trying (to put it lightly) years of our lives. But I've seen a lot of changes in all of us as the "sewage" gets taken care of. I can't wait till the major overhaul is done!

I'll never forget the day, last week, when I started crying out of the blue and you just held me for so long. God healed a place inside that needed His touch badly while you were holding me.

I can't really explain how I felt. It kind of made up for the times I needed that long ago and didn't have it.

I'm so thankful for our friendship . . .
Love,
Laurie

During this time of healing, we were still experiencing a continued lack of peace with some people. As I began to think more clearly, I was also able to be much more objective.

The decisions that are made in a case like ours are unavoidably going to affect many people in as many different ways. Everyone will have at least slightly differing philosophies. No matter how things are handled, someone won't like it. When a baby is involved, the situation is emotionally volatile. Any number of sparks can set a blaze going.

We had been right to assume that if we consistently asked God to guide us, He would be a solid support all the way through. But beyond that, our expectations were, indeed, naïve.

Our emotions and energy were directed very much toward Laurie and what was happening to her and her baby. So it was easy to read acceptance into everyone's initial reaction. When the rumors began drifting in, they were easy to ignore, too. Second-hand information usually *is* best ignored.

People seemed so understanding. But we never should have expected them to understand. *We* hadn't understood anything about what it would be like until it happened to us. We were also naïve to expect that *people* would readily forgive our failures. True, we all received total and complete forgiveness from God. But some people never would be able to grant that mercy to us.

On the other hand, God was very good to give us many people who *were* supportive, whether they agreed or not with the decision made. They helped us cope with feelings of rejection and unworthiness as we walked through that difficult time.

"What pointers would you have as people relate to an unmarried, pregnant girl and her family?" I was asked one day. I had to think about it for a while, then came up with these four suggestions:

1. *Ask God to help you not to be critical, judgmental, or condescending.* This is especially difficult for people who have never fallen into open, sexual sin, people who have no children, or whose children are still young. It is very easy to make judgments concerning the "obvious reasons" for a girl's pregnancy and wrongfully placing blame.
2. *Communicate.* The suffering family, no matter how well adjusted, will feel very much alone and will have a lot of guilt feelings and self-examination to deal with. They will need people to talk to, and to listen to them. Be aware of the decisions that are being made. If you honestly disagree, prayerfully and lovingly tell them so.

   Don't tell the family about negative statements made by other people. Instead, encourage the others to come to the family themselves. Point out to the critic the fact that those who may have insights the family lacks bear part of the responsibility for the situation unless they share those things directly.
3. *Be supportive.* Whether you agree or disagree with decisions being made, be a friend. Give your love and prayer support. Even if you can't find it in your heart to be supportive, refuse to gossip or speculate with others.
4. *Continue to communicate and be supportive after the baby is born.* Whether the mother keeps her baby or not, the family will need people who are willing and unembarrassed to face reality.

Our thoughts were occupied with the lessons we were learning. On top of that, life continued to be full. We both knew that our daughters wouldn't be at home for much longer. Except for Carina, of course! Lynn had been away at Bible school all year and was due home soon. She had a real desire to just be with her family for a while.

Dawn would be leaving home to go college the next fall, and we sort of expected that Laurie would go back to Bible school in the fall, too.

Knowing all this, we'd been giving most of our attention to our daughters. It was delightful.

Tom had bought a new camera and was a photographer for Dawn's track team. Carina and I attended most of her meets, and I was involved in all the plans for her senior class functions.

Instead of pursuing another living situation just yet, we parked our bus at Tom's parents' house. They lived much closer to school and jobs and to the church we attended.

Tom and Carina and I slept in the bus, and the girls each had a bedroom in Grandma's house.

We ate all of our meals in the bus and had good family times together. How kind of the Lord to give us this special, healing time with our children. How exciting that they, at their ages, wanted to be with us!

16
LORD, SHE'S ALL YOURS

Laurie continued to go through many changes. Her attitudes, habits, and emotions were being "plowed up" and reworked. Even her attitude toward Rick was being dealt with. I'd noticed a difference when she spoke of him. One day I asked what had brought that about.

"Well," she answered thoughtfully, "it's a continual process. Every time I think of him, I'm learning to *let* myself think about him, instead of getting upset and putting him out of my thoughts. I look right at him in my mind, then I forgive him and bless him." She smiled. "It gets easier every time. Of course," she added, "I finally had to come to the place where I took full responsibility for my own actions, too. I know I can't blame him for everything."

Laurie had seen Rick a couple of times since the baby's birth. Things had been awkward at the first encounter. The second time they met was by chance in a shopping mall. Laurie showed Rick a wallet-sized picture of Elise Joy and offered it to him. But he refused it and said he'd call her. She could send him one.

"I knew he wouldn't call," Laurie said later. "He was curious to see what she looked like, but he doesn't want to live with it." There was no anger in her, only sadness.

But later, he did call. He and Laurie had lunch together and he admitted his own hurt and feelings of loss. He asked for a picture and went out and bought a frame for it. More healing and understanding came through that interaction.

Another friend Laurie hadn't seen for a while was Dave. They had shared so much while they'd been at Bible school that she still missed him a lot.

Dave had been writing to her, with the help of friends, and Laurie was always delighted to get his letters. After reading one of those letters, she had a sudden inspiration.

"When is that retreat going to be up at Deception Pass?" she asked. "I'd like to invite Dave to come down and go with us. He speaks to groups all the time, you know—shares his testimony."

And so Dave spent a few days with us, staying in a cabin with our family. Everyone was immediately drawn to him, and we enjoyed watching him enjoy himself. He swam and played with everyone else.

Laurie and Dave had a long talk and reaffirmed their friendship. But they agreed that anything more than a friendship was not what God had for them. It surprised us that we all were so sad as we put him on the bus to go home. Such an easy person to love!

Laurie's emotions were mixed when the day came that she received news that Dave was getting married. But she was truly happy for him. God had even given him a wife who was a nurse. She would be able to give him the physical help he needed. God considers everything.

"I'll always be grateful for our friendship and for the things I learned from him," Laurie said tearfully when she heard the news.

One situation at a time, all the loose ends were being tied up.

Laurie had also come to grips with her use of food. She used it less and less for comfort as her life took on more meaning and direction.

Part of this "direction" had to do with unwed mothers. Ever since the birth of her baby, Laurie had been spending time with other girls who had been, or were, pregnant. Some were referred to her by the adoption agency, others by friends. These girls needed a friend who understood, and they found that understanding in Laurie.

Gradually, Laurie became stronger and more confident, and discovered that it was a two-way street. More healing came through her relationship with these girls.

So much had been happening that, in a way, it seemed as if years had passed since Elise Joy's birth. But on the other hand, it seemed like only yesterday. I was amazed one day when I glanced at the calendar.

"She's a year old today!" I said out loud to an empty bus.

Later, Laurie came in and sat down.

"It's a special day, isn't it?" I asked softly.

Laurie nodded. "I think I want to finish my letter to her and send it in a birthday card."

I wondered, was she really ready to let go yet? It would still be hard, and I prayed that God would bless her writing.

That evening Tom and Carina and I had to go out. When we came home, Laurie and Dawn were waiting for us.

We walked through the door and in the middle of the table was a lovely German chocolate cake. There was one big, pink candle on top.

Laurie and Dawn grinned at us.

"It's about time!" Laurie said, laughing. "We've been waiting to have a birthday party!"

We sat down and Laurie lit the candle. She waited a few minutes, made a wish, and blew out the candle.

Nobody cried while we ate the delicious cake. But I couldn't help thinking about little Elise Joy having her first birthday party. I wondered what kind of cake her parents had baked.

Of course, they couldn't know our family tradition. Each child was given a chocolate cake on the first birthday. After the candle was out, we would let the birthday person dig in—literally! Then the cameras would flash and record a very messy child for future enjoyment.

I let my thoughts wander ahead to a day, seventeen years from now, when Elise Joy would be given the letter written by her natural mother. I prayed that there would be no bitterness, only love and understanding as she read that lengthy letter. Parts of it flashed through my mind.

> Dear Elise Joy,
>
> Hello. I hope you don't mind me calling you by the name I chose for you. I don't know how else to start this. . . .
>
> There are so many things I want to say to you, I don't know where to begin. It's strange to be writing to you, knowing you are a part of me, maybe something like me in looks, talent, or personality, and yet I don't know you. Hopefully this letter will help you to get to know me a little. . . .

Laurie continued, sharing all the important, big and small, details of her background and life. She didn't want her daughter to have any unanswered questions about her heritage.

She even wrote about the birth.

> You were born in a birthing room. As you came into the world you had quite an audience. It meant a lot to me that so many people were there. They supported me, and opened themselves up to my pain.
>
> The second you were born, a wave of peacefulness like I've never felt came over me. Peace stayed with me all night and through the next day.
>
> I held you on my bare stomach for half an hour, talking to you and looking at you from head to toe. Your eyes followed every move I made. You even smiled at me when I blew in your face accidentally.
>
> While I held you, Jesus reminded me that I'd loved you and given you everything I could. I'll never forget the joy and peace that overwhelmed my heart at that moment.

I had been afraid to love you for a while during my pregnancy. I didn't know how. I thought that if I loved you I'd become more attached, and it would be harder to let go.

I began to learn to trust Jesus; I knew that He had it all in control. Then I was able to let myself become vulnerable by loving you, knowing I couldn't keep you.

Because I love you I ate right, took care of my body and prayed for you. I delivered you naturally so that I could be fully aware of the different stages of labor, and I would know when you were actually born.

Now and for the rest of my life, I can look back and know that through Jesus I gave you a beautiful beginning. I shared a part of your life that could only be experienced by me. Through God I was able to make the most of what we had together. We shared everything as a mother and daughter that God had planned for us. . . .

You're a special lady and God wanted you to be born into this world. He's got an extra-special plan for your life. I wish I could watch that plan unfold. I would love to be a part of it all. But Jesus has something else in mind for both of us.

I miss you. I often long to hold you, to be your mother. But I know you're in the right place. I know you're with the family God had for you even before you were conceived. You're not with them by chance. God gave you to each other through me. I am privileged to be a part of that gift. . . .

Laurie had planned to finish her letter by Elise Joy's first birthday when it would be sent, through the adoption agency, into the adoptive parents' keeping. But she was still struggling to actually end the letter.

Finally, one day about three months after her little girl's birthday, Laurie put the last pages into my hands.

> . . . It has been hard for me to finish this letter. I've been working on it for over a year now. I was hoping to get it done by your first birthday, but it didn't work. I just don't want to say good-bye.
>
> Your birthday was very special to me. It was a peaceful day. Sacred is a better word. I even made a birthday cake in your honor. My family and I all ate cake together, quietly sharing in the celebration of your life.
>
> There is so much more I could say. I'd like to go on forever. I've wanted to tell you everything I would ever want to say to you. I know that's impossible. I'm sure there will always be something I'll wish I could tell you.
>
> I want to share with you all my good times, hard times, struggles, victories, and failures, because I want you to know me—so that I can somehow encourage you. Maybe even help you to understand yourself a little better. I guess I'm trying to do part of what I would want to do if I were your mother. I'm seeing now that to try to do that any further than I already have is not my place. Now that I've realized that, I can finish and feel at peace about it.
>
> I want you to know, beyond all the detail and facts, that I really love you. I loved you while I was carrying you, I loved you in an even deeper way as I held you, and I love you now. You will always hold a very special place in my heart. No one else can take that place. I will never forget you or purposely banish you from my mind.
>
> Please don't ever think I didn't want you. Sometimes I want you with me so badly all I can do is cry. Something inside feels like it might burst. But no matter how much I miss you and want you

to be with me, I have never regretted or felt that I made the wrong decision. Even in the times I hurt the most, I have a peace inside that will never leave. God has blessed me with the peace of knowing you are where you belong. I can always hold on to that.

If you ever want to find me I want you to know I am open to that. Whatever you're comfortable with. It's your decision.

A letter doesn't seem like much when you wish you could be so much more to someone. Don't forget I'm also praying and thinking about you. Whatever you go through in your lifetime, don't ever lose sight of God's love for you. He is our only reason—

I love you,
Your other mom

EPILOGUE

It's hard to believe that nearly two years have passed since my little girl was born. The peace God gave me concerning my decision has remained, hasn't wavered. I continue to see Him working steadily in my life, and I can still confirm all that is written in this book.

Yet I have struggled with something I couldn't quite identify until now. As I read through the book, toward the end I begin to pick up a subtle "happily-ever-after-story" feeling. No matter how slight this may be, I don't like it.

I've read too many books that have left me awed but discouraged, because "I could never be like that!" I have trouble identifying with a person who appears to have all the solutions tied up in a nice little package.

Because of this undefined pressure, I've found myself trying to live up to an image of myself that I have in my mind. You know, I *should* be totally healed, pain-free, continually joyful and victorious.

What I *really* want, though, is to be genuine. It was my intention and prayer that, as you read this book, you would see, above all, that God can take any person and any circumstance, and He can change, restore, and heal. But if anything is to be gained from seeing this, it must be understood that healing is a *process*. Growth is a lifelong affair—something I pray will continue until the day I die.

I still hurt sometimes. Every once in a while something will trigger painful feelings that surprise me. A mother with a new baby. An off-hand remark. I have to stop long enough to acknowledge the hurt and experience it. Then more healing comes. But it takes time.

Occasionally, I still find myself using food for comfort. There are scars from broken relationships, lingering fears, and weaknesses.

I want you to be able to identify with me, to know that I live where you do. I'm not "all better, fixed up, neat, and tidy." But God is changing me. The healing recorded in this book is just the beginning.

God is allowing things to happen just fast enough for me to be able to handle them. As each occasion arises for me to be in the public eye, I find that my faith has been strengthened enough to see me through.

God is faithful and gentle. As long as I find my strength *in Him* I'm OK. He never asks anything of me that He hasn't prepared me for. And He'll be just as good to you.

—Laurie Lewis

Part Two

BITTERSWEET

. . . The Restoration Continues . . .

17
THE "LOOK"

Mom," Laurie whispered, "do you see that guy sitting up in the front row?"

I followed her gaze and nodded.

"Well, he really loves Jesus."

"Have you met him?" I whispered back.

"No."

I looked at him again. He sat leaning forward in his chair, elbows on knees, chin in hands, obviously very attentive to the pastor's words.

Later that afternoon Laurie and I were cleaning up after lunch. She was humming a little tune as she wrapped up the remains of the sandwich that Carina had left behind in favor of "helping" her dad do something or other outside.

"By the way," I asked nonchalantly, "what do you know about 'that guy' you pointed out at church this morning?"

She put the wrapped sandwich in the refrigerator, and answered me without looking at me. "His name is Timothy Carr, and he works with the youth at church." Then she shut the door and turned to face me with a wry smile. "And don't worry. I've just been watching him. From a distance."

After Laurie's baby was born, she dated someone for a while. But it wasn't long before it became obvious that she was once again yielding to the old needs for belonging and significance. She was still craving affection, needing to be special to someone. There was yet an empty, needy place in her heart. "Mom," Laurie admitted one day, "I finally let myself see that I've fallen for the same, empty solution once again." She hung her head, then looked at me mournfully. "Can you believe he already had a ring?"

I hugged her, and when I let her go there was a resolute look in her eye. "I'm sick of this. I need to learn to let God's love be enough for me. Meantime," she announced rather vehemently, "I'm swearin' off men."

And indeed, the next six months were a man-free respite. She was determined to wait for the one God had for her and not settle for second-best just to ease her lonely, aching heart.

"Something inside has just shifted," she told me, smiling slightly. "I have made peace with my design as a person, with who God made me to be. I'm sensing affection and acceptance from God in a way I never have before." Her smile broadened. "I'm even beginning to like myself!"

Laurie kept herself busy working at a restaurant and spending time with her sisters and cousins, and of course, she and Carina were inseparable. I could see even more of God's plan in sending that little girl to us at such a late date. He knew that not only did we need her, but Laurie did, too.

"Guess who came to the restaurant this afternoon?" Laurie grinned as she relaxed after work one day. "Timothy came in with the worship pastor from church, and they were seated at one of my tables. So I said, 'Hi, I'm Laurie Lewis, and I go to the same church you do.'"

The two men were happy to meet her and said, "We were just discussing a conference that we're going to in California."

At home we had already talked about that conference, and Tom and I were planning to go. We had asked Laurie if she would like to go with us, but she had no interest.

"We are both going," the worship pastor told her as she gave him coffee. "You should go."

"Yes, I think maybe I should," she answered.

Then she resumed her duties, and they finished their food and left.

A few weeks later, Tom, Carina, and I traveled the twelve hundred miles to southern California in our bus. Laurie drove a car down, planning to spend some time with cousins after the conference. We met at the huge church where the conference was to take place. Laurie had Denise with her, a girlfriend from Bible school. When we were parked, Tom and the two girls headed toward registration. Carina and I stayed in the bus, and I began preparing lunch.

About an hour later, the trio returned.

"Laurie, have you been in the sun too long?" I asked. Her cheeks were red, and she looked somewhat dazed.

Denise rolled her eyes. "Instant, fumbling attraction," she muttered disgustedly.

"What's going on?" I demanded. Laurie fell into a chair and Carina climbed all over her. She buried her face in her little sister's hair.

Piece by piece the story came out. The three of them were in line to register, and within seconds, Laurie spotted Timothy ahead of them. Before long he turned and actually *saw* her for the first time. He told us later that when he looked at her, he saw a glowing light over her head.

That "look" was a bolt of lightning for them both. For the rest of the week they kept "bumping into" each other, having brief, instantly forgotten conversations. She often found him looking through the crowd at her, not too discreetly, not glancing away very quickly. Denise saw the looks, heard the inane conversations, and kept rolling her eyes.

During the noon break one day, Laurie brought Timothy to the bus for lunch.

"Well, hi!" I greeted him. He smiled warmly, green eyes twinkling, and I knew I'd love him. Yes, I could see what the physical attraction was. Timothy was a handsome, rugged, California boy. But beyond that he had a compassionate, tender heart, a genuine love and concern for people, and a passion for God. As we ate lunch together, I had the strong impression that this would not be the last meal he shared with us.

When Timothy left to return to the conference, Laurie wandered to her bunk and lay down for a few minutes' reflection. At the time she didn't share her thoughts with me. But later she said that her only thought, as she lay there staring up at the bottom of the upper bunk, was, "Oh no. I am probably going to marry this man."

Timothy's parents lived near the church that sponsored the conference. Though we didn't know about it then, he went to his mother and said, "Mom, I've found her."

Tom, Carina, and I drove the bus home, and, as planned, Laurie stayed behind, planning to visit cousins and friends, taking a week to get back. A couple of days later we received a colorful, California-beach postcard from Laurie. It was a rather incoherent message, something about being on a date at the beach with "this incredible man!" and discovering that they were "made for each other!"

Timothy returned to Seattle right after their afternoon date at the beach, and Laurie arrived home, as planned, a week later. She was tanned and glowing. She looked at me, eyes wide. "What if it's all a dream? What if I'm reading more into this than I should?"

Then they saw each other again. It was no dream.

One day, after they had spent the afternoon together in a park by the water, Laurie came to tell us an amazing story.

"I wondered what was wrong, because Timothy began to get all nervous and twitchy. Then he suddenly blurted, 'There's something that I have to tell you, Laurie. I left home at sixteen, married at nineteen, got divorced a year later, and I have a little boy. His mother remarried, and her new husband adopted Shawn and doesn't want him to know he is adopted. So I can't be in his life at all.'"

I gasped. "So what did you say to that?"

"I said, 'Well, I had a little girl when I was eighteen, and I gave her up for adoption.' Then we laughed and cried together, marveling at the ways God had known our hearts, our losses and fears, and brought us together in such a specific, amazing way." She smiled, her eyes sparkling with tears. "God answered the secret cry in both of our hearts, to be known and loved in spite of our failures."

One week later, on the Fourth of July, two weeks after "the look," Timothy took Laurie to a gorgeous spot at the foot of nearby Snoqualmie Falls and asked her to marry him. She said yes.

18
SEEING DOUBLE?

"Y ou're *what*?!" Lynn shrieked.

"We're engaged, Lynnie." Laurie held out her left hand to show Lynn the sparkling ring on her finger.

"But you *can't* be!" Lynn had been waiting for a ring from Barry for almost two years, and here came Laurie, engaged in two weeks!

"I hope you're not planning on getting married before we do," Lynn warned.

"Well," Laurie almost whispered, "we might."

"Laurie! I'm gonna kill you!" Lynn and Barry had been talking about a Christmas wedding, and Christmas was only five months away.

Laughing, Laurie found me to tell me the news. We were in a local park with other family members, having a holiday picnic. I was sitting on an air mattress while four-year-old Carina played nearby with a couple of cousins.

I smiled as Laurie walked up, long, blonde, curly hair glowing in the sun.

"So how's Timothy?" I asked.

"I have something to show you." She looked a bit hesitant. She stuck out her hand, and there was a beautiful ring. It didn't register at first. I thought, *Oh, that's a pretty extravagant gift so soon in the relationship.*

Then it sank in. I lay back on the air mattress in shock. I am a true romantic, but this seemed awfully fast, even to me.

Tom, however, didn't take it lying down. After all, this was his little girl. And hadn't we just been to hell and back with her? He wasn't about to hand her over so easily.

"Well, he never asked me," Tom said in response to the big news. "Tell him to come and talk to me."

Oops. In their exuberance, they had overlooked a bit of protocol. The details of that meeting are between Tom and Timothy, but the result was confirmation of the engagement.

Meantime, Lynn and Barry became officially engaged, Lynn was wearing a gorgeous ring, and they began planning for a wedding on December 29. Laurie and Timothy didn't really want to wait that long, though there had been some discussion about a double wedding.

I was sitting in the yard with Lynn and Laurie one day, thinking about bringing up the "double" idea again, when Lynn asked, "Mom, do you think all those masses of poinsettias will still be on the platform in the church by December 29?"

"I don't see why not," I answered. "They will probably keep them through New Year's."

"Oh, good." Lynn smiled. "It'll be beautiful with the guys wearing black tuxes and the girls coming down the aisle in red velvet skirts and white satin blouses, carrying long-stemmed, red roses." She sighed. "Very elegant, don't you think?"

Elegant indeed. "So, Laurie, what are you envisioning?" I asked.

"Well, what I really want is silver-gray tuxes for the guys, and full, lavender taffeta skirts with off-white blouses for the girls. And I'd love to have them carry baskets of dried flowers. We could decorate the candelabras with dried flowers, too, lavenders, pinks, dried grasses."

I had a one-second, horrible vision of the combination of these two scenarios. From that moment on there was no more "double" talk.

A few days later Laurie and I were chopping vegetables for a salad, when she casually announced, "Timothy and I have decided to get married on November third."

Happily, I didn't chop off any fingers in response.

My mind raced. November 3 and December 29. November 3 is less than four months away. December 29 is less than eight weeks after that. Two big weddings. Same church. Same preacher. Most of the same guests. Four daughters in each wedding. Same father-of-the-bride. Same mother-of-the-bride . . . of the brides.

"You OK, Mom?"

"Of course," I managed. "Why do you ask?"

Laurie pointed at my very large pile of chopped carrots.

"I like lots of carrots in the salad, don't you? Crunchy."

The weeks that followed were a blur of shopping trips, of trying on countless, very different, wedding dresses, of deciding on fabric for the attendants' dresses for both weddings, of looking for invitations, of sampling wedding cakes, and of trying to check off a respectable, daily number of other items on the interminable lists.

I planned to arrange all the flowers for church and table decorations as well as the personal bouquets. Fortunately Laurie's could be done ahead because they were dried. And Lynn would only need personal flowers because of all those blessed poinsettias.

Carina was absolutely thrilled. "Mommy! I get to be a princess two times!" Nothing could have been more exciting for a five-year-old who loved to play dress-up.

Her mother wasn't quite so thrilled. I hate dress-shopping for myself. I can never find anything I really like. Lynn and Laurie tried to help but finally grew exasperated.

"Mother! We give up," they finally told me after I'd turned up my nose at several dozen of their findings.

Working alone, I became obsessed with finding the perfect lavender dress. Each time I entered a store, every lavender dress in the place would jump out at me. Eventually I did find something I could live with.

Walking out of the store with the lavender dress, I tried to adjust my thinking for the job still ahead of me. "Think red dress. Think red dress. No more lavender—think red."

The weeks flew by. We received incredible help from family and friends, with food and organization and sewing the many dresses that needed to be made. Then November 3 was upon us.

We all know God loves weddings. After all, Jesus' first miracle on this earth took place at a wedding. Since then, He has performed many miracles at weddings. There is no other explanation for the transformation that takes place the minute the music begins, and the first participants venture down the aisle. No matter how frantic and/ or chaotic things might have been a few moments before, suddenly the magic happens. The miracle begins.

After I was escorted down the aisle in my lavender dress, candle-lighters illuminated the scene flame by flame. Silver-gray tuxes shone in the warm glow. Smiling beauties floated down the aisle, full, taffeta skirts swishing softly. Then came a broadly smiling Princess Carina in her hand-made, lace-trimmed, be-ruffled, floor-length, lavender taffeta gown.

Suddenly I was standing and turning for the glorious moment that makes me cry at every wedding. But this time I was the mother-of-the-bride. My vision blurred as the handsome, smiling father-of-the-bride appeared with an exquisite, veiled creature on his arm. She held her head high, walking in purity, and wearing her forgiveness like a crown.

Our daughter, Laurie, of whom we were very proud.

19
WAITING AGAIN

Nine months later Carina and I drove from Seattle to Laurie and Timothy's home in Southern California. Our goal was to arrive before Laurie's honeymoon baby put in an appearance. Laurie's due date was ten days off, but I didn't trust my very pregnant daughter to stick to a schedule.

"Mommy, are we here?" I had barely slipped the car into park when Carina was already unfastening her seat belt. "Is this Timothy and Laurie's house?"

"We're here, Carina, we're here." I laughed. We had made good time, and were several hours ahead of schedule. Laurie greeted us warmly, and we all hugged with giggles and tears. Carina and I poked Laurie's tummy and laughed.

As soon as we were inside, Carina began a tour of inspection. Watching her, Laurie's mouth dropped open. "Mom!" she whispered "She's so tall!" And more tears came.

"And Laurie, you're so huge!" I reminded her. "You've both grown."

We followed Laurie around the spotless apartment. When the tour was over, we went to the overstuffed car to unload boxes of odds and ends I'd been collecting for weeks. We sat on the floor while Laurie unpacked and exclaimed over everything. There were late-arriving wedding gifts, presents for the baby from relatives, lots of baby clothes, stuffed animals, a lamp.

"Oh. I know what this is." Laurie smiled as she pulled a soft, pink, zippered bag out of the bottom of a box. "Carina's 'little girl' baby clothes." She set them aside without looking at them. "We'll see," she murmured.

"I'll take them home with me if it's a boy," I told her, but I knew it was a girl.

Timothy came home from work, and I remembered all the reasons I'd missed my new son almost as much as I'd missed Laurie. I watched him with her, so tender and thoughtful. His heart showed in his eyes.

For the next week, while Timothy was at work, we three girls had a nice vacation. We talked and talked as we sat by the pool and watched Carina turn into a fish as she learned how to swim. I was so grateful that this time Laurie could rest in her motherhood, knowing that the pain she would soon experience would only be labor pain. No signs of that, yet, though she did have a doctor appointment.

Laurie and Carina and I drove to the doctor's office and met Timothy there. He liked to be in on all of her appointments since he would be coaching her in the delivery. He and Laurie went in, and Carina got busy inventing things with colorful, plastic, snap-lock blocks. We watched other mothers and babies come and go. I was very anxious to hold my new granddaughter in my arms, and I didn't care if knowing it would be a girl seemed presumptuous.

Timothy knew it was a girl, too. Laurie didn't allow herself to think "girl," though I knew she was continuously reminded of her first pregnancy. And her first little girl. I, too, was remembering. My care-free seventeen-year-old having to grow up so quickly, and being forced to make such earth-shaking decisions for one so young.

Laurie was twenty-one now, almost twenty-two, and fully a woman. We'd been remembering together all week. I'd recalled the searing pain she experienced at giving up her child at birth and marveled again at the sacrificial choice that had been hers alone to make. But

I also remembered the peace God had given her, and I still saw it in her.

"I can hardly believe it," she exclaimed. "After this delivery I'll actually have a baby in my arms!" She told me about the many ways God had been healing old hurts with each stage of her pregnancy. And this time she had Timothy.

My reverie was cut short as the objects of my thoughts walked into the doctor's waiting room. As usual, Laurie's protruding stomach appeared first, then the rest of her.

"I'm dilated 4 centimeters and 85 percent effaced," she announced. "The doctor says not to go anywhere without my supplies."

Ah, the plastic bags. They were all packed, with towels, pads, baby things. Then there was the brown paper bag of coach's supplies. "Timmy's Bag" as Laurie had labeled it. In it were a Bible, some honey (for energy), a package of breath mints, and other goodies. All I had to remember was to get the ice chips and frozen juice out of the freezer and put them in the ice-chest when the time came. Oh, yes. I also was supposed to call the doctor when Laurie's contractions were about eight minutes apart.

Timothy kissed Laurie good-bye and went back to work. In the car I told her that several of my babies had arrived right after a visit to the doctor's office. On the way home we finished shopping for the last few baby items. The laundry was all done. The car was washed. I'd trimmed Laurie's hair. She was ready.

"My worst fear is that I'll have this baby on the freeway in the middle of rush hour traffic," Laurie admitted. The thought didn't thrill me much either. The knowledge that both Timothy and Laurie were trained for an emergency delivery was somewhat comforting, but anything could happen on the forty-five minute drive to the delivery site.

"Oh, by the way," Laurie remembered, "the doctor thinks I'll have a really short labor.

"Good," I answered, at the same time silently praying, "Lord, let it be longer than forty-five minutes please.

By 9:30 P.M. all was calm. Laurie and Timothy were asleep, but Carina was full of energy in spite of the fact that she had spent her usual number of hours in the swimming pool that day.

"Carina, you'd better go to sleep. We might have to wake you up in the middle of the night, you know."

"I know," she answered happily. "I might be an auntie tonight."

20
THE TREASURE

Carina finally fell asleep beside me. I knew I should be sleeping, too. I got up and opened the bedroom door a little, got back in bed, and watched the ceiling for a while. But sleep finally came.

I woke to muted voices. Then I heard Timothy and Laurie's bedroom door open and here came that tummy again. When Laurie appeared, I whispered, "What's happening?"

She calmly told me that she had awakened at 3:00 and had a few strong contractions five minutes apart. Then they were four, and now were coming three minutes apart.

I was on my feet. "What time is it now?" I gasped, grabbing my clothes.

"It's three-thirty."

"Good grief. Did you call the doctor?"

"Well, no. I wasn't sure. I mean I hate to wake him in the middle of the night if it's a false alarm."

I looked her in the eye. "Is it a false alarm?"

"No."

The doctor told Timothy, "I'll meet you in the office in forty-five minutes."

Laurie sat and laughed at Timothy and me as we fell all over each other trying to get ready to go. Get the bags. Pillows. Ice-chest. A blanket for the car. Oh, yes, my shoes. Carina! But first I carried what I could to the car.

Someone had parked behind the car and it didn't look like I'd be able to get it out. But I jockeyed back and forth and finally eased out past the offending pickup truck. Then I dashed back upstairs to get Carina while Timothy deposited Laurie in the car.

"Carina, Laurie's having the baby! Let's go."

She was awake immediately, and out of bed, but wobbly. I picked her up, wrapped a blanket around her and carried her down to the car, dumped her in the backseat, and crawled in beside her. Timothy drove and Laurie sat in the front with him. As her labor progressed, I wondered if maybe the two of them should be in the backseat. Just in case.

For most of the trip Laurie was relaxed and still laughing at us. Then she got quiet. After a few minutes she said, "That one was stronger."

I realized I was unconsciously stepping on an imaginary gas pedal. "How much farther?" I asked as nonchalantly as I could manage.

Finally we pulled into the parking lot. "Here we come!" Laurie sang. It was almost 5:00 A.M. Dr. Marchbanks appeared in the office doorway as we got out of the car. I hadn't seen him before. Laurie was right. He did look like Santa Claus, belly, white beard, and all. But instead of a red suit, he was wearing pale green scrubs.

Timothy hurried Laurie inside with Carina close at their heels. She was still in her nightgown, long, blonde hair tousled. I opened the hatchback and hurriedly pulled everything out. Timothy opened the office door just as I reached it, and took the supplies. Carina was impatiently waiting in the doorway to the warm and inviting birthing room.

Pretty flowered sheets covered a double bed with a curving, white, rattan headboard. The room was lit by soft, indirect lighting that drew attention to delicate, restful murals on three of the pale-blue walls.

Laurie and Timothy settled right into their practiced routines. After a few minutes Carina got bored and headed for the waiting room and the blocks. Following her, I met Santa Claus in the hall. He smiled warmly.

"You are awfully cheery so early in the morning," I commented.

"Well," he explained, "God always prepares me for these births. Last night I had the worst sleepy spell right after dinner, so I went to bed at 7:00. Woke up at 3:00 this morning. I was wide awake when Timothy called." He patted my arm and went to check Laurie's progress.

A little later I peeked through the open door. Timothy was reading the Bible to Laurie, and she was resting between contractions. As I walked back toward the waiting room, I heard the two of them weeping softly together. I knew that God was present in that room with them, and that healing was taking place that could only happen through another birth experience.

A nurse named Barbara arrived to help. Carina and I cuddled on the couch while I read her a book. But my ears strained toward that room. Finally I couldn't wait any longer.

"Carina, I think we'd better get back in there. It sounds like that baby is getting anxious to meet us!" We hurried through the door just in time to hear Laurie say "I think I need to push."

There was a sudden flurry of activity. Barbara ran to get the doctor and then brought a foam rubber, wedge-shaped, back support and propped Laurie up. Laurie was at the bottom of the bed, and Timothy was beside her. The doctor sat on a low stool facing Laurie with her feet on his knees. Carina sat cross-legged on the floor beside the doctor. The camera and I were looking over Laurie's right shoulder.

Contractions came strong and fast. The first two caught Laurie a bit by surprise. "Hold your breath, honey!" Timothy commanded. "Grab your knees and push!"

Laurie obeyed, and pushed with all her might as she had the third and fourth contractions.

Carina jumped to her feet. "It's a girl! A girl!"

A beautiful, perfect, slippery, funny little girl. We all laughed, cried, hugged each other, and passed the Kleenex box. It was 6:05 A.M.

"God is so good. God is so good," Laurie murmured. "A girl."

Barbara hurried into the adjoining bathroom and began filling a huge tub. Dr. Santa Claus did all the necessary fussing with Laurie and the baby while the water ran and ran. A normal tub would have overflowed long before. Finally it was ready. Timothy helped Laurie walk to the bathroom and she climbed into the tub. The doctor handed her the baby, Briana Rochelle. Then Timothy joined them. He was prepared, having worn his swim trunks to the office.

The celebration began. Cameras flashed as Timothy, Laurie, and Briana luxuriated in the warm water.

"It feels so good I may never get out," Laurie warned.

There was room for three or four more people in that huge thing, but somebody had to take pictures. Carina knelt at the side of the tub, beaming at the new little family.

It was finally time to pull the plug on the party. When they got out of the water, we took more pictures. Mommy, Daddy, and Baby. Daddy and Baby. Mommy and Baby. Carina and Baby. Doctor and baby. Granny and Baby. Baby.

We gathered up all the supplies we hadn't had time to use, and discovered that one item was missing.

"Ummm. . . . I forgot my pants." Timothy faced a wet ride home, but Dr. Marchbanks came to the rescue with a pair of his green, Santa-sized, drawstring pants. Timothy gathered them around himself, and we all laughed.

At 8:25 we were in the car and on our way home. By 9:15, we had Laurie and Briana in bed, and I was fixing a special breakfast. Timothy and Laurie sat in bed and ate breakfast from a tray. Omelet, toast and jam, fresh fruit, and juice.

Carina and I sat in the living room, sleepy but contented.

"Carina, wasn't that special, watching Briana being born?"

She looked up at me, smiling sleepily, and whispered, "I'll treasure it forever." Then she added, "She's a treasure."

I agreed.

21
MULTIPLE CARR FAMILY

In a hot tub?!" I hollered into the phone. "You say he was born under water?" I sat down to hear the rest of the story. I deduced that Laurie had truly enjoyed that great big tub after Briana was born and decided to give her second-born a swimming lesson right off the bat.

"Michael Timothy Carr," I repeated, smiling. I shed a few tears, too, because I was so far away. We were living in Maryland, working at a private retreat center on the Chesapeake Bay. Timothy and Laurie were back in Washington State.

As soon as we could arrange it, we made a special trip back to meet our first grandson. While there, we realized that things were not going well for Timothy and Laurie. Timothy didn't seem to be the person we remembered, and at first we thought perhaps it was simply that he was realizing what a heavy responsibility he had, in his growing family. We soon understood that it was deeper than that.

"Timothy's brokenness from his past has really come to light," Laurie told us. "I looked at him one day and thought, *I've bitten off more than I can chew. Who is this man?* I think we need help."

A few months later, at our encouragement, Timothy, Laurie, Briana, and Michael came to Maryland, and we shared a house for about a year. Carina was so very happy to have other small persons in the house, and Tom and I loved the opportunity to spend concentrated time with our children and grandchildren.

The retreat center was actually an old farm estate right on the bay. What an adventure for all of us. It was a wonderful place for the children to roam and play, though Michael did manage to knock out one of his brand-new front teeth on one of our kitchen chairs.

There were nineteen cats in the barn, some of which Carina adopted. There were big turtles to capture and snakes to admire or scream at. Carina drove a miniature, gas-powered Model T all over, sometimes with a small passenger. The huge swimming pool saved us on the days when we sweltered in the humid heat. And there were tons of bugs to collect.

In his pain, Timothy's greatest desire was to hear from God, and to find answers in his struggle. At one point, he believed that the Lord was telling him to learn to play the guitar. Because none of the rest of us had thought he had any interest in music, I'm afraid we were pretty skeptical. The skepticism grew as he persistently and faithfully worked away at it. But God was faithful, and soon Timothy was doing quite well. The rest of us began to truly enjoy his playing. Briana and Michael loved listening to their dad and mom play and sing.

During that year, Timothy also received wonderful counsel and friendship from special friends of ours who lived in a nearby town. He definitely started down the road to his restoration as we spent the last few months of our time in Maryland.

Eventually we returned to Seattle and the Carrs stayed behind. Things seemed to have smoothed out for them, at least temporarily. When Andrea was born, we were in Seattle and the Carrs were in Virginia. This time we traveled the other direction to meet our new granddaughter.

Meanwhile, Dawn and Lynn, and their husbands were adding to the population explosion. Lynn and Barry kept moving from one state to another following his job. Dawn and Stan settled on the east coast, where they had met.

The Carrs returned to Seattle with their three children, and we shared a house again for a while. Then they moved to a nearby town and proceeded to add to their fleet. When Jadon was born, I was there. I'll never forget sitting on the bed beside Laurie, during the home delivery. I was encouraging those last, mighty pushes.

"You're almost there, Laurie!" I joined the chorus of advice from Timothy and the midwife. Then, suddenly, a brand-new little boy popped out, right into my lap!

Timothy and Laurie continued to have their ups and downs, but Laurie never said too much about their struggles. They came to live with us again, once more in a transition time with job and house. This time, we finished an apartment on the lower floor of our home for Tom and me and had two separate households.

We enjoyed the privilege of watching the children grow and mature. There was always a sense that God would not leave unfinished the work He was doing in the Carr family.

Timothy and Laurie both continued to pursue their musical passion, and worship music often filled our home. As the children got older, none of them needed to be urged to try their hand at music in one form or another. They watched their dad, who had become a skillful guitar player, and their mom, who played keyboard and sang.

One by one, the kids began playing on their own: guitar, bass, keyboard, drums in their own distinct styles. They began writing their own music and producing it. The family played and sang together on many occasions. Music and worshiping God was, and would continue to be, a constant through the years.

In retrospect, we could see clearly that even in the midst of deep struggle, Timothy had truly heard from the Lord about learning to play the guitar. And the reward for his obedience was a family with a passion for music and for worshiping God together. What a heritage he had passed on to his children!

One day when Jadon was about four years old, Laurie came downstairs with news. "Guess what?"

"How many guesses do I get?" I asked. She had that "look" in her eye again!

A few weeks later, sitting across the room from Laurie, I began staring at her burgeoning tummy. "Laurie, how far along are you?"

"I know." She smiled wryly. "I'm not as far along as I look." She patted her belly and mused, "Maybe I'm just really stretched out. After all, this is the sixth time around, you know!"

But that tummy kept expanding and expanding, until all of us were sure something was different this time. Laurie became the constant topic of conversation. Finally, when she was six months pregnant, she convinced the midwife that she needed to have an ultrasound.

Andrea, Michael, and Briana, went with Laurie to her ultrasound appointment. The three of them stood quietly along the wall while the test was done. The technician was watching the screen intently, and suddenly asked, "What did you think you were having?"

"A boy," Laurie answered.

"Well, it looks like you have two girls in there!"

At her words a large gasp ricocheted along the row of children. Laurie had a sudden vision of two beds, two highchairs, two of everything. When she had recovered enough to be mobile, they went to the store to buy some balloons and then came home to tell Timothy and the rest of us. Actually, one look at the twin balloons Laurie had tied onto the back porch rail told the story, and they didn't have to tell us anything. There was great excitement that night.

It was stunning to watch my slim daughter morph into such a huge one! We kept track of her amazing measurements as the weeks passed. A week after the ultrasound, Laurie went into premature labor and spent a week in the hospital. A very kind-hearted nurse finally saw that Laurie needed to go home, and arranged for her to do so.

We set up an adjustable bed in our living room and tried to keep Jadon from climbing on his mommy too much. Laurie had to administer regular shots to keep her babies inside as long as possible. For two months she lay there, and we watched her grow. Carina painted Laurie's toenails and shaved her legs for her, and Timothy took the kids camping a lot to give her periods of quiet. We made a ritual of recording her measurements and then taking a picture every week to track the expanding size of her belly.

It was an emotional period of time. Tom's dad was dying, and we were trying to spend time with him. Carina helped out with the children, and we did what we could between visits to Grandpa.

"Laurie, Grandpa is gone." I spoke into the telephone at the nursing home. "I'll tell you more later, but he died with a smile on his face."

The next day several of us were around Laurie's special hammock in the yard, talking more about the events of Grandpa's death. Laurie seemed uncomfortable and asked Timothy to help her to the bathroom. I shook my head as she eased off of the hammock and clumsily maneuvered into the house and to the bathroom.

A few minutes later the bathroom door opened and Timothy announced, "Her water broke! It's happening!"

A call to the midwife set things in motion. It had been decided ahead of time that Laurie would go to a large hospital in Seattle because of the fact that she was having twins and because of the complications. Soon Timothy, Laurie, and I were in the car on our way. We called Carina, and asked her to go to be with the older children. All of us were glad to be in motion, but not terribly worried as we headed toward the hospital.

When we arrived at the door, Laurie was admitted and taken to a delivery room to settle in and let nature take its course.

Then Laurie stood up. It took a second to realize what I was seeing. The floor beneath her was a pool of blood. The next moments were a blur as everyone leaped into action. Laurie was whisked into an operating room as people flew this way and that. Her doctor had not arrived, so another was hijacked in the hallway.

Timothy tried to follow her, halfway into his scrubs. They took Laurie through two sets of swinging doors, leaving Timothy and me on the outside. One of the twin's placentas had abrupted, or ripped loose. They were going to do an emergency cesarean.

Timothy looked frantically through the small window in the door, and then found the large button on the wall that said "Open." He smacked it and hung through the doorway until the door began closing, then smacked it again. He finally figured out how to make it stay open, but it all became too much for him, and he lunged

through. Then he practically ran through the second door which was
also open.

I was afraid they would throw him out, but he never reappeared.
Suddenly a nurse burst out of the room with a tiny bundle in her
arms and ran down the hallway. A couple of minutes later, a second
nurse did the same, carrying another bundle.

All was quiet in the operating room, and from where I was sitting,
I could only see reflected blurs on the window of the open door. I'd
been praying like crazy for Laurie and her two little babes.

Finally the emergency was over and things were under control
enough so that they could fill me in. There were two little girls,
Alyssa and Arianna. They were somewhat preemie, but not much.
Arianna was having a bit of difficulty with her breathing because her
lungs weren't fully developed, but there was every reason to believe
that she and Alyssa would both be fine.

When I saw Laurie, she was calm and peaceful, though a little sad,
knowing that she would probably have to leave her babies in the
hospital for a while. The twins stayed there for ten days, and we made
many trips in to see them and hold them.

"It kills me to leave them here," Laurie said tearfully after one of
those visits. I knew that she couldn't help but think about another
little girl she had left behind. But I reminded her that Arianna and
Alyssa were being left just as much in God's hands as Elise Joy had
been.

There was much rejoicing the day that we brought the two little girls
home. All of us assumed that this would be the "Grand Finale."

22
SHAWN

"Mom, I just wanted to run something by you," Laurie said one day. "Oh, and ask you to pray for Timothy."

That was something I did pretty regularly, pray for my kids and their husbands and offspring, but I could tell that this time something was up.

"As you know, Timothy went surfing yesterday."

He went off by himself occasionally to get some time to spend alone with God. As the father of six, his responsibilities had multiplied, and he was wise enough to know when he needed to de-stress. I had heard him leave early the day before, and prayed for him as he drove out. As much as it worried me to know that he was surfing alone in the cold Pacific, I also believed that God did use those times to speak to his heart.

"So, did he have a good time?" I asked.

"Yes, but here's my concern. When he got home he said to me, 'Laurie, I believe that God told me that I would be reunited with my son in October.'" Laurie paused. "Mom, there are only two days left in September. I guess I'm afraid of how he will react if it doesn't happen."

I promised to pray, hoping that Timothy had really heard accurately but not having a whole lot of faith that he had understood. "Lord, protect his heart. Prepare him for whatever You have planned."

For eighteen years Timothy had honored the wishes of Shawn's adoptive dad and not tried to see his son. As far as he knew, Shawn didn't even know he existed. There had been some contact between Timothy and Shawn's mother, a step toward restoration. But his adoptive father still did not want Shawn to know he was adopted. The pain had been unbearable at times, and Timothy prayed constantly for his oldest son, that the Lord would be his true Father. Timothy and Laurie continued to find comfort in the understanding each could offer the other.

Three days later, I looked out my window to see Timothy's truck head out the driveway. Laurie came running downstairs.

"Mom! You will never guess what happened!"

My heart nearly burst and my eyes overflowed as I listened to her tell the story.

"This afternoon the phone rang and I answered it. Some guy asked 'Is this the home of Timothy Carr?' I said yes and gave the phone to Timothy.

"Timothy talked for a few minutes and hung up. He had the funniest, dazed look on his face. Then he said, 'That was Shawn's roommate.' He said Shawn had suddenly, out of the blue, asked him to find his dad. The guy is a skip-tracer, somebody who finds missing persons, and it only took him a half hour. Timothy looked like he didn't really believe it yet, and said, 'Shawn wants to meet me.' Then it was like he came back to earth, and his feet hit the floor running! He grabbed a few belongings and threw them into the car. Now he's on his way to Idaho." Laurie finally stopped to breathe, tears spilling down her cheeks. "I'm so happy for him!"

I hugged her, awestruck. Oh, me of little faith. "I am praying that their reunion will be wonderful."

The hours dragged as we waited to hear from Timothy. It was like being in the middle of a really great book, and having someone snatch it and run away with it just at a riveting point in the story. I went through the motions of my day, jumping every time I heard Laurie's phone ring.

Finally Timothy did call, and Laurie came running downstairs. Her eyes were leaking again, and my heart sank, but only for a second until I realized they were tears of joy.

"Timothy got there before Shawn was even home from work," she said. "He was there when Shawn walked in the door. Several of their first hours together were spent in the park, playing their guitars and talking to homeless guys." She laughed and continued, "It's incredible!! They have never known each other, yet they both love to surf and skateboard. But the most wonderful connection is in the fact that they both love to play the guitar, and both have a heart to worship God. After the park, the two of them went to a prayer meeting that Shawn regularly attends and met with about fifty kids. Shawn and Timothy led the worship together, and then the two of them prayed for people. Shawn's friends got to see God's restoration first-hand through his reunion with Timothy."

I was speechless. And oh, so thankful.

"And guess what?" Laurie said excitedly, "Shawn is coming back home with Timothy to meet the rest of us!"

When the two of them walked into our house, we hugged them, then stood back and began staring. Shawn looked so much like Timothy it was startling. He was taller than his dad and blonder but built the same and had very similar features. He also looked just like his newfound brothers and sisters.

As time went on, we saw more and more similarities. One of his traits made us laugh hilariously. We had always been amused at Timothy's propensity for mixing metaphors, and making up words that sounded so right it would catch you off guard. One of our favorites was, "Put that in your hat and smoke it." And now, here was his son, apart from him for twenty years, doing exactly the same thing!

Shawn became a permanent fixture in the family. A miracle of restoration. Laurie immediately welcomed this "new" son, and rejoiced with Timothy in the joyful reunion.

"All these years we couldn't bear to even speak the name Shawn because it brought so much pain," Laurie admitted. "To be able to just say 'Shawn!' is so healing, and to be talking back and forth and easily using Shawn's name is awesome. His coming into our lives is the beginning of deep healing, the rumblings of change."

The days that followed weren't always easy as Timothy tried to understand how to walk with this person who was his flesh and blood, his son, but not raised by him. There were all kinds of regrets, things he wished they could have experienced together. Now his son was an adult, and Timothy was trying to understand what that adult needed from his father. Sometimes when Timothy and Shawn were together, they would both get very moody, but their relationship grew as they learned together how to be father and son.

Restoration also came between Timothy and Shawn's mother and adoptive father. Forgiveness for long-ago hurts was granted and relationships mended. A new sense of responsibility was growing also. As Laurie put it, "When your children, who have been lost, start returning to you, it calls you to a higher place. Makes you consider how you are living your life. Makes you want to live it more fully and with more integrity."

I thought about Shawn and how well he fit into the Carr family. Besides looking like all the rest of them, he had a similar personality and blended seamlessly into the crew. They all loved him dearly.

"I've never felt that Shawn has taken anything away from the other kids," Laurie said. "He only gives. He has added something to our family that has been missing from the beginning."

But, as thrilled as Laurie was for her husband, I knew that, as time passed, she had to wonder once in a while, "Will it ever be my turn?"

23
"DEAR DAUGHTER . . ."

can't believe that she'll be eighteen years old in eight days!" Laurie's face reflected a combination of sorrow and joy for the daughter she hadn't seen since her birth. She held out three handwritten pages, and I took them, wondering.

"It's a copy of the letter I finally wrote to Elise Joy. It's taken me all these years to be able to say what I wanted. It'll be notarized and put in her file at the adoption agency. I thought you might want to read it." She turned and went into the next room, leaving me to read in privacy.

> Here I sit, Monday evening, all the kids are in bed. Timothy (my husband) is staying at his parents' house for the night. It's actually quiet, and I can't quit thinking about you. I've composed letters and songs to you at different stages over the years, never completed, tucked away in my journal.
>
> I remember a time when you were turning fourteen, and I was especially burdened in prayer for you. What was going on? Will I ever know?

I had the impression at the time that though you knew in your head you were loved—are loved, you still had the question deep in your heart, "If you loved me, why did you give me up? If my own birth mother could give me up, how could I truly be loved? Am I lovable? Am I worth loving, completely, for who I am?"

I am wondering about the repercussions in your life because of the choices I made almost twenty years ago. Scary. At this moment I have a measure of doubt over my choice. However, as I held you, and looked at you then, I had a deep sense of peaceful conviction that I was doing the right thing.

Because I was trusting in God for both of us, and I believed that He would lead me to the right choice, I didn't doubt through that time. God was, and still is, in control of both our lives, leading and loving us to the right places. Though I often take detours, He is still bigger than my failures and stubbornness.

So—what I'm feeling today, I guess, isn't really doubt so much, but grief. Loss. Ache. I expressed some of my thoughts to my father tonight. He, with cotton in his mouth because he had a tooth pulled today, said, "Regardless of the emotions that come up, the truth is that you made your decision under the guidance and direction of the Holy Spirit and He led you into what the Father had intended for both of you." Comforting words from a very wise and wonderful man, cotton and all.

I'm glad you were born and I know you made two (at least) special people very happy. That makes me glad, and I hope and pray that you have known the love of God in a real way.

I've wondered throughout the years if we might have met and not known it. Or if I knew your parents somehow. What do you look like? Do you have my blonde hair, my smile? Are you tall? Do you sing as I do? Do you cry easily? Are you stubborn like me? So very many questions . . . so much to tell . . .

My husband works in construction, but our real passion is music—worship and song-writing, born out of a heart to be closer to God and to take others there with us.

My dad, your grandfather, carries a picture of you around in his wallet and prays for you as he is reminded by your sweet face. You were Mom and Dad's first grandchild, and they consider you so always. They number you along with the other twelve—proudly, I might add!

I respect your family and the life you have. I admire and am thankful for your parents. I have no desire to unsettle any of you or disrupt what is happening in your lives. But I want you to know I welcome you into my life at whatever point you have the desire—if you have the desire.

You have brought a depth and richness to my life that I would not have had if you had not been born. I thank you and I love you.

Your mother at birth,
Laurie Carr

24
THE QUIVER FULL OF ARROWS

"Any news yet?"

Laurie spoke into the telephone, asking Carina the question they had been repeating to each other daily.

"No. You?"

"No. But I'm really suspicious."

"Oh, Laurie! Wouldn't it be fun to be pregnant together?" Carina and Matthew had been married for two and one half years, and Carina was eager to join her three sisters in motherhood. The timing was a little less than ideal because Matthew was getting ready for three months at boot camp with the National Guard.

Immediately after their conversation, Carina went to the grocery store and bought a dual-pack pregnancy test, hurried home, and tested herself. Moments later she was on the telephone telling Laurie the very exciting news.

"Carina! I can't wait to see you. I'll be there tomorrow, and we can celebrate."

The next day Laurie and her kids made the hour-and-a-half drive to Carina's house, and they all rushed in to congratulate her. When the excitement died down a little, Carina remembered that she had bought two pregnancy tests.

"Laurie, do you want to use the other one?"

The celebration that followed was a double one.

On December 21 Carina and Matthew's son, Nico, was born. Laurie was there with the rest of us, encouraging Carina through a very long, difficult labor and delivery. I saw Laurie rubbing her own large tummy occasionally and knew it had taken courage to stand and watch. I briefly wondered if we might have two babies that day!

But, Miss Amber Laureen Carr arrived ten days later on New Year's Eve and became number seven in the growing Carr family.

When both babies were about two months old, they were dedicated in a double ceremony at our church. Afterward we all went to a baby shower at Auntie Tia's house. During the party, Laurie and Carina sat nursing their babies. Laurie was watching as Nico quickly filled his tummy so full he was wheezing.

"I don't think Amber is getting enough milk," she said. "She wants to eat all the time and she is so fussy, even right after she nurses." She frowned. "It makes me sad."

Later, Carina fed Nico, and after he had gorged himself, she fed Amber. The little girl latched on and nursed voraciously. Laurie cried. When Amber finally couldn't hold another drop, she passed out into a deep sleep, limbs flung wide, her little face the picture of satisfaction.

After a short discussion, Laurie and Carina knew they had a "together-job" to do.

Laurie and the children moved in with Matthew, Carina, and Nico temporarily. I helped out, and life for the two mommies became an endless round of changing diapers, nursing, pumping, eating, and then starting all over again. It seemed that Carina was constantly either nursing or on a pumping machine. Both babies flourished and the moms enjoyed each other's company immensely,

Lynn and Dawn came to meet the two new family members, and get a "baby-fix." Dawn didn't know it yet, but she was a few weeks pregnant at the time. Those girls definitely liked to do things together. When Laurie and the children returned home, Carina continued to pump and send as much milk as she could to little Amber.

The Carr family moved to Virginia while Amber was still a baby. Once again, Timothy hoped new places and new people would fix all that was wrong in his life. He was still searching for the answer to his restless quest for the person he wished to be, trying to run away from the person he thought he was. He was in so much pain emotionally that he had to constantly do something in a desperate attempt to avoid facing himself.

With this move, he and Laurie left behind a house they had been purchasing, and it went back to the bank. It was very hard for Tom and me to watch them go once more, knowing that their financial situation was getting critical. But, again, we knew that the deepest cry of both their hearts was to find God's best for them, and we prayed for mercy.

The move to Virginia didn't work out the way they'd hoped circumstantially, but it marked the beginning of the end of Timothy's constant emotional cycling. When he realized that Laurie was close to the breaking point with his constant job changes and need to relocate and the chaos it caused the family, he knew that he had a choice to make. He could continue to live out his own pain and erratic lifestyle, knowing that if he did, he would probably lose his wife and family, or he could stop running from himself and learn to live as the redeemed and loved son of God that he was.

They moved back here to Seattle and stayed with us while they worked through a year of crisis during which Timothy struggled for wholeness. In the process he learned something very important and wonderful about himself. He couldn't run from his "father-heart." He loved his children desperately, and it was his deepest desire to just be a good dad to his kids.

Laurie told me simply, "Timothy chose love."

But Laurie still had a lot of "stuff" to deal with herself. In the hubbub of family life around us as we lived together, Tom and I didn't recognize the depth of the pain that Laurie was experiencing until later, when she told us some of the thoughts she'd struggled with.

"I came back from Virginia feeling a lot of shame and a huge sense of failure as a Christian and a wife. I was so angry at my husband that I even felt a growing hatred toward him. You and Dad have always seemed so stable and consistent. I would make comparisons and that was unbearable. I had no idea how depressed I had become."

During the months they spent with us, the prayers and the faithful, listening ears of some dear friends helped bring healing and understanding as Timothy and Laurie opened up to them and faced the issues in their lives. Later, Laurie was able to articulate more of the reasons she had struggled so much.

"For the past fifteen years, there were months at a time when we would be OK. Then Timothy's cycle of self-hatred and his feelings of insignificance would close in again. He would be overwhelmed by the heavy responsibility he carried for me and the kids and feel totally incapable of the good he wanted to do. He'd have this job, then that job. We would live here, then there. Things would be right, and then wrong, right, then wrong. Over and over again."

She laughed ruefully. "Of course our problems weren't all one-sided. God's been teaching me to put my hope in Him and stop expecting my husband to fail. I need to help him succeed. Now I can see that even in our weakness and failure, God was working in our family. There's been a flexibility instilled in all of us that has prepared us for whatever He eventually wants us to move into."

We watched them go back to the east coast once more, this time walking into restoration in the process. Once there, they began to see the fruit of their desperate love for God and for their children, which had always been intact and powerful through all the peaks and valleys, the years of wandering and searching. All of the children were moving in their musical giftedness, and all were growing and thriving in their relationships with God. They were following Timothy and Laurie's example of always trying to put God first in their lives, even though their parents had failed miserably at times. Basically, God was answering the cry of two desperate parents: "Please keep our children close to Your heart."

We received a tape-recorded message from Laurie, passionately describing the changes she was seeing in her husband:

"I've known he's loved me all these years, and I've loved him. But the evidence of his love has increased so much in this past year as I've watched him lay his life down for me. In little and big ways he has served me. He has loved the rebellion and mistrust right out of me.

The ways he cares for our kids and allows me to find time for myself, putting me first, has healed my heart."

Then she talked about Psalm 127:5, which says, "Sons are a heritage from the Lord, children a reward from him. Like arrows in the hands of a warrior, are the sons born in one's youth. Blessed is the man whose quiver is full of them."

"Children really, really are arrows. I guess we needed a lot of them!" I could hear the laughter in her voice. "People say, 'How do you do it with so many kids?' And my thought is, *How would we have done it without them?* They are truly our arrows. Each one has brought a different strength to us. Then when Shawn came, he brought a Shawn-shaped arrow."

Her voice wavered as she went down the list of names. "Briana, Michael, Andrea, Jadon, Arianna, Alyssa, then Amber, all of them were arrows—when we needed them."

She was weeping now, but she struggled on. "And Elise Joy. She is an Elise Joy–shaped arrow. Oh, mom, children are not a burden. Why do people think that? Children are a gift and a heritage. And a great reward."

She had to stop for a moment, then continued.

"People look at my life and think, 'I don't know about her. She's got all those kids. That's crazy. Don't they know how it happens?' I hear that *all* the time. It seems like our world thinks backward in so many ways. Every one of our kids is a reward and has brought strength to our lives, and we need them."

The tears took over momentarily, but she had more to say.

"I don't know—I don't know how our kids are turning out to be such amazing people! We are told that children need stability. They need to have 'things' around them to keep them feeling constant, to hold them." She laughed a little. "It must not be true, because our kids have lived so many different places and have lost their belongings and their friends and their homes and their pets—but God has kept them.

"And I don't know how it's happened. I don't know! It's wild. But how could they be who they are today except for God's hand in their lives? I think the best thing that we've given them, that's kept them, is a desire for God. We've not given up even though we were feeling ashamed of who we were and feeling like failures so many times in church and family relationships. But in spite of all the inconsistencies, there was one constant thing in both Timothy and me. We couldn't quit going after the prize, this treasure that we were constantly seeking. We knew, over the years, that there was more, that God was bigger, a better Father than we could imagine. We knew that He had more in store for us and we couldn't give up.

"As the kids grew older, we'd look into their faces, especially as they became teenagers, and we could tell that they were really starting to see our weaknesses, insecurities, and instabilities. We had to grow, because if we didn't, they wouldn't grow either.

"So, in spite of it all, because of God's mercy, these guys have what they need, and they are becoming all that they were meant to be. I'm proud of them. And I am so thankful."

25
IS IT TIME, LORD?

September 2, 2005 was a beautiful fall day. Tom came into the house, handed me the mail, and went back outside. I began absentmindedly sorting through the stack. As usual, most of it was garbage.

I picked up a long white envelope, and was surprised to see that it was addressed to "Laurie Lewis Carr." When I glanced at the return address, my eyes flew wide open. It was from an adoption agency, and I immediately knew.

I raced for the telephone. It seemed to ring forever. *Are you ready to have your life changed forever, honey? Again?* I was misty-eyed as she finally answered.

"Laurie, are you sitting down?"

She chuckled. "Well, I was chasing Amber, but I'm sitting down now. What's up?"

"I'm holding a letter from an adoption agency. It's addressed to Laurie Lewis Carr."

There was silence while my words sank in.

"Do you want me to open it?"

"Yes!" she answered before I got the question all the way out. I ripped open the envelope.

> Dear Laurie,
>
> We are an adoption agency in Seattle. We are trying to locate a person by your name regarding a very confidential matter. This is not an emergency but if you believe you could be this person would you please call me?

I gave her the telephone number and hung up in a hurry so she could make the call. Then I paced near the phone until she called back.

"Mom, it's true. It's about Elise Joy—my daughter. But her name is Clare. She grew up in Vancouver, Washington. That's all I know."

The tears let loose, and I began asking way too many questions at once. "So will you be talking to her? And when? And when can you meet her?"

Laurie sounded a little frustrated. "They won't really tell me anything. They said the first step is for her to write to me. Through them. I don't know why on earth they didn't seem to know how to find me. I put all our contact info and pictures in with the notarized letter I took to them for their files a couple of years ago."

"So now we wait?" On the one hand, we had already waited for twenty-four years. Why did the prospect of waiting even another twenty-four hours seem unbearable?

"I guess we don't have any choice," Laurie said softly. And the waiting began.

The months passed, and though we didn't ever say it, we were all wondering what was happening in Clare's life. Maybe she was dealing with some difficult things, or maybe she had changed her mind and decided that she didn't want to go through with the meeting. But that was too painful to think about, so we just waited, trying to do it patiently.

In the midst of the waiting, joy kept cropping up in many places. Briana brought a large portion of joy to her parents by presenting them with a future son-in-law. One more arrow for the quiver! Briana and Gabriel's January wedding brought us together again, this time on the east coast. It was so much fun to see the whole family all dressed up and a part of the beautiful occasion. Laurie was stunning in a long, silky, green dress. She looked more like a bridesmaid than the mother of the bride, let alone the mother of eight children.

Four times I had been escorted down the aisle as "Mother of the bride," the last time just six years earlier at Carina's wedding. It was different to walk down the aisle on the arms of two tall grandsons, and sit in the left front section to witness the first wedding of a grandchild.

I was surprised by the tears that began as the Jewish shofar was blown loudly to signal the beginning of the ceremony. Both Gabriel and Briana were eager to put Jesus in the center of their marriage. They were also including some rich, Jewish traditions from Gabriel's background, and a rabbi stood beside the pastor.

Of course we cried as the beautiful bride came down the aisle on her father's arm, and again as our son-in-law spoke riveting words of love and blessing to his daughter and son-to-be.

"The words that I have to say are a heritage from the promise that the Lord gave me, when He restored me and gave me a wife and many children," Timothy said. "Briana was a reward to me, and Gabriel, today I give her to you. Unless the Lord build the house, those who labor, labor in vain. Stand together and watch the favor and prosperity of the Lord. This day may you two be blessed as you start your journey in a heritage of promise. My blessings are on you."

As the ceremony progressed, I watched Briana's face for signs of discomfort and nervousness. She is a very private, quiet person, and I wondered how she was handling being the center of attention among several hundred people.

Once Timothy sat down, Andrea began singing a beautiful song she had written for the two of them: "Captivate Me." Gabriel stood in front of the platform, facing us and watching Briana as she approached him. She then began slowly walking around him, her long train following her gracefully. Her eyes locked onto Gabriel's and his followed her as far as possible without his spinning in a circle himself. Then he quickly turned to watch her come around the other

side, as they gazed again at each other. Once . . . twice . . . three times
. . . seven in all.

We knew that the new couple had decided that the traditional kiss
in the wedding ceremony would be their first kiss ever. I expected that
moment to be very emotional, but I wasn't prepared for the "circling,"
which symbolized the binding of the two together and the creation
of a new family circle. We were totally undone as we watched, feeling
as if we were intruding on a very holy moment. Our shy Briana's face
was transformed, radiant and completely unself-conscious.

She held her head high and smiled serenely as she seemed to float
around Gabriel. It was obvious that she was seeing only him. I didn't
know whether I could bear to continue watching, but I lived through
it, and through the beautiful ceremony, and the vows they had written for each other. And then the kiss. Their first kiss.

Gabriel and Briana married under a canopy, called a "chuppa,"
a symbol of their new home together. After the ceremony, Gabriel
stomped on a cloth-wrapped glass, reminding them of the fragility of
life, and that broken wedding vows are not easily mended.

Later, at the reception, the live band played Jewish dance music,
and everyone formed a circle around Gabriel and Briana. They
both sat on wooden chairs and were hoisted into the air by several
strong young men. Up and down—up and down, as the dancers
circled. They smiled and waved as they flew past each other. What a
celebration.

I know that Laurie's heart was singing with thanksgiving and joy
as she watched her second daughter marry the man she loved. I was
sure that she'd had more than a fleeting thought in the course of the
evening, as I had, of her oldest daughter, Clare, yet unknown.

Five months passed, and I knew that sometimes Laurie had dark
days when she wished that she didn't know that her daughter had
initiated a search. One day in February she simply sat down and
wrote a short letter to her and sent it through the agency:

> Dear Clare,
>
> This whole letter thing is awkward, isn't it?
> Getting started is the hardest part for me. I
> am so glad you initiated contact with me. I have so

much to tell you, but that's not the purpose of this letter. I really just want you to know that you are constantly on my mind and I would love to know you and see you. To hear/see who you have become and learn what your life has been like. To meet your family, if they want to, and say "thank you" to them for receiving you as their own (I know that wasn't hard).

God allowed me to be a mother in this life and you are one of my children, though you are a grown woman and the details of who you have become are established and I've not been a part of those years.

All that to say I also feel the tension or awkwardness of this, but more than that, just a desire to know you. I am in South Carolina and plan to be on the west coast this summer with my family. I also would gladly fly out to meet you before then.

I would like you to write or call me directly if you would like to, and have the adoption agency drop their role as middle-man.

Peace and Grace to you, Clare.

(I love your name)

Much love, Laurie

Three more months passed. Suddenly it was May 15, just past Mother's Day. When Laurie called, I assumed that she was calling me to say, "Happy Mother's Day" a day late, because they had been out of town.

Her voice was unusually quiet. I couldn't quite tell what she was feeling all those three thousand miles away. But, as with that life-altering "Mom-I'm-pregnant" phone call twenty-four years before, I knew that something was up. Just then Carina got on the extension phone.

"Laurie!" she greeted her sister happily. "What's happening?"

"I got a Mother's Day card today with a wonderful letter from Clare!" she told us with some difficulty.

My heart leaped and I wept as she described that beautiful little card to us.

"And there are pictures."

It was all I could do to keep from demanding that she go immediately and copy the pictures and send them however they would get here the fastest! But I had to be satisfied for the moment with her description.

"She's beautiful. And I think she's tall. She's built like Carina, but she has dark hair."

Joy welled up. She was back. God was returning the little girl we had put into His hands for safe-keeping twenty-four years before.

"I wish you could see this card." I could hear Laurie's smile. "It's a smallish, old-fashioned-looking card. There is a bouquet of pink roses and lilies of the valley on the front, with a circle of blue forget-me-nots in the center, surrounding the word *Mother*. Inside, it says 'Happy Mother's Day to the one who gave me life.' There are three pictures of her in the card."

How I wished that she could somehow transmit the pictures through the phone! She didn't have a scanner, so I knew it would be a while before we saw them.

"Should I read you the letter that came with it?"

"Silly question!" I shot back.

I curled up in my big, blue chair, and hugged the receiver to my head, eyes closed, and savored every word.

    Dear Laurie,

        I have to admit it feels a little strange addressing this letter to "Laurie." It sounds so distant or foreign to me because for so long, even nameless, you have meant so much more to me than a mere first name address would imply. I guess I will leave that for time to solve as I hope it will.

        I'm THRILLED to be at this juncture in my life, as I have so long waited for the day that it felt right in my heart to find you and to know you. I always knew I wanted to, but I didn't want to push it; wanted it to be a natural progression within me and also right in conjunction with the chaos my life has been as of late. It's a big, beautiful mess, and I love it, but there has been a lot to work through. That is the wonder of it all, I suppose. There's plenty of time for me to tell the story of my life since you graciously released me into the arms of my mom and dad, who are incredible. God has touched my life so sweetly through my parents. I'm a blessed and lucky girl and I know it.

Since learning more about you in September, I found *Bittersweet* on Amazon.com, bought it on September 3rd, had it by September 10th, read it by September 10th PM. I cried my way through that one! I have become so much more aware of God's plan in my life through it, and through those of my family, including yours. I had never really had a true testament to my faith until I read that book. It's incredible.

And here I am now, on an eastbound train from Portland to Spokane to go see my little sister, Valerie, at college. Mountains and fog, rivers and waterfalls, bridges, trees and sky—and I, all contemplative and missing you somehow.

I'm in awe of all of this—in awe of you, of this process and of the watershed of emotion this has already tapped inside of me. It's as if I didn't have access to this entire portion of my soul previously, and now I can finally see in.

Thank you for writing to me. As soon as I saw the Agency envelope, I knew what it was. I know the handwriting, and the 'For Clare' gave it away (I've read your first letter a million times.) I want to meet you, and soon.

My mom tells me a story about a time in my life when I was really struggling, three years old, and telling her she wasn't my mom, throwing plenty of tantrums. One day we were together, doing nothing special, and I said this:

"You're my mom and you're gone.

My mom's gone because she loves me.

My mom's gone and she brings me sunshine.

My mom's gone and she brings me a penny.

My mom's gone, and she's here."

That was the end of the troubles. I understood, as I do now. And you ARE here. And I love you.

Love, love, love,

Clare

Amazingly, the Mother's Day surprise had come nine months from the time Clare began her search. Another birth? A few days later Laurie mailed a letter to her daughter.

Dear Clare,

Wow. Now it's my turn. You surprised me. I received your letter the day after Mother's Day. We had just returned from a four-day event in Atlanta. Otherwise I would have received your letter right on Mother's Day!

I began to weep as the reality of what I held in my hands sank in, and as I pulled out your pictures, a huge wave of emotion came. All these years of waiting, wondering, hoping for a future, yet always laying it down. And right here—now. . . . There you are. The timing is, of course, amazing, and shifting something deep inside me.

You are beautiful . . . BEAUTIFUL . . . incredible and I can't wait to see you face to face. You look like me, my sisters, and my older daughters. Strange mix of familiarity and mystery!

Your letter completely took my heart—you have an amazing gift in writing. I've read it and reread it as I have stared at your pictures over and over. I can't tell what your eye color is!

There are ways that you express yourself and things you touched on that remind me of me—the way nature causes your contemplation, the way you let your heart out. How many times over the years have I sat staring at the ocean, aching inside, wondering what your life was like, who you were becoming. Your letter totally wrecked me—in a good way. My heart is feeling things I haven't allowed, and I so badly want to fill in the details.

My life is crazy, and I loved your comment about the chaos of your life—"a big, beautiful mess." I hope you don't feel like you have to figure it all out or have everything together (is that possible?) before we meet. I've been through a lot and my heart is not judgmental. I'm figuring out plenty of my own stuff.

There is so much I want to say, but I really just want to get this in the mail so that you will know how happy I am to have heard from you. John 16:21 talks about a woman, when she is in labor has sorrow . . . but as soon as she has given birth to the child, she no longer remembers the anguish for joy that her child has been born into the world. Jesus was comparing this sorrow to His leaving the earth. The next verse says, "You now have sorrow, but I will see you again, and your heart will rejoice and your joy no one will take away from you." There has been sorrow, but there has been joy along the way, and I am rejoicing now.

If I felt it would not overwhelm you, I would get on a plane tomorrow—what do you want? . . . Please don't feel pressured. I want to move how you want to.

As I said so many years ago, I loved you then. I loved you as I carried you, held you. I've loved you through the distance, and I love you now.

The words you said to your mom at age three were so profound and healing to me. I know that was God speaking through you as well as to both of us.

I love you and look forward to your reply. We could also e-mail if there is anything immediate you want to say.

Love, love, love back to you—
Laurie

After Laurie mailed her letter, the e-mails began to fly back and forth.

I'm too excited about all this, Laurie. ☺

I just received your letter and pictures, and I have to say that I have not been able to stop looking at them for a minute. And I've been showing you off to all the people in my life who know even a little about my story. It's just so amazing to look at you and see someone that I share genes with—not once in twenty-four years have I seen another human being who I look like because I'm supposed to look like them. Obvious statement, I know :) but it's an amazing thing. And your letter was perfect! I have blue green eyes, by the way. With a kind of amber circle around the pupils which looks like I may have gotten that from you.

I don't want you to have to spend an arm and a leg to get out here. Let me know what you are thinking though. I will be checking my e-mail left and right so we don't waste any more time.

Love love love,
Clare

. . . God doesn't do anything halfway. He is a wise, happy God with many surprises up His sleeve, if He has sleeves. I also show you off—still—can't help myself. I carry your pictures in my purse/journal. Anyway I have eight year olds (did you know you have twin sisters?!) trying to make crepes . . .

Love you,
Laurie

OH my goodness the joy in my life just gets greater every day. I had heard something along the way about twins but little twin girls! :) I can't even imagine. All these siblings to meet! They must be so beautiful. Have you ever had crepes with Nutella? That stuff is straight from heaven (add bananas if you're really hungry). Like you said, He doesn't do anything halfway, and I don't want this to turn into one big week(end) where we meet and then aren't really a part of each other's lives. NOT that I think that will happen—I just want you to know how excited I am to know you and grow with you—to continue our story. THRILLED about meeting those that are close to you, family and friends, the more the merrier and the more of a blessing.

Love you,
Clare

In June, nine months after that first letter from the adoption agency arrived, we picked up Laurie at Seattle-Tacoma airport. She looked different somehow. The last time I'd seen her, there had been no Clare in the picture. If I'd had to describe the way she looked, I would have said there was an aura of expectancy about her. It was almost like the glow of pregnancy, but with the slightest bit of uncertainty in her blue eyes.

Tom and I both gave her long hugs. She looked young and trendy. Her slim body and youthful haircut didn't give away her age or station in life.

The next day we sent her off in our car to make the four-hour trip from Seattle to Portland. She had originally expected to stay with friends and then meet Clare at some agreed-upon place, but Clare wanted her to stay in her apartment. So, a little shaky in the knees, Laurie decided to make the trip by herself. I had a lump in my throat as I watched her drive away.

"Lord, give her a peaceful trip and no awkwardness when they meet." I knew that was a big order, but we have a big God.

"Find out if she'd like to come meet us," we'd told Laurie. "Don't pressure her, but if she's interested, we'd love her to drive back with you and visit for a day or two. We'll pay her plane fare back to Portland."

None of us really expected her to want to come. After all, it really had to have been a huge thing just to meet her birth mother without having to deal with a bunch of other family members.

Then Laurie called. "We're coming!"

When Laurie had cautiously broached the subject, Clare responded immediately, "How soon can we go?"

The following hours were filled with excitement and almost a sense of disbelief. Was it possible? After all the years of hoping for this day, could it really be here? But we didn't have time to sit around and wonder. There was a barbeque to plan. It was a beautiful, sparkling, sunny, Seattle day, and we planned to eat outside. Lynn and Barry were there with their kids, James, Rachel, and Mari. Matt, Carina, Nico, Tom, and I were all on hand as well, to meet our Clare.

I found a roll of white paper and got out the marking pens. The kids helped me make a large banner to hang across the vine-covered arch in the front yard where Matt and Carina had gotten married. It was angled just right so that Laurie and Clare would see it as soon as they pulled into the long driveway.

We hung it up with two shades of pink crepe-paper streamers on each end, blowing in the breeze. The large letters announced, "WE LOVE YOU, CLARE!"

26
"I'VE FOUND MY TRIBE!"

T hey're here!" The lookout did his job and brought everyone running from different parts of the house and property. Our van had
paused at the end of the driveway, and I'm sure they were taking in
the scene of the place where Laurie had grown up and so much family history had been made. A new chapter was about to be written.

The car finally came up the driveway and rolled to a stop. The
passenger door flew open and a tall, slim, dark-haired girl flew out
and into our arms.

"At last!" I cried when it was my turn. It felt like I was hugging
Carina. Clare wore a blouse in one of "our" favorite colors, corn-
flower blue, and everything about her seemed very familiar.

I kept my wits about me enough to take pictures of a number of
those first hugs, and then during the rest of the afternoon. We sat
outside, stared at each other, talked nonstop, barbequed, ate together,
compared various peoples' features, and looked at photo albums. It
felt as if we were only scratching the surface. There were so many
years to catch up on.

"I started crying as soon as I saw the banner!" Clare told us. A combination of big, Cheshire Cat grins and tears seemed to be the order of the day for all of us, sometimes both at once.

Laurie and Clare spent the night a few blocks away at Lynn's house, sharing a bed and giggling together like schoolgirls. They simply couldn't get enough of each other fast enough.

The time passed far too quickly. Way too soon, we had to put Clare on a plane back to Portland. We were left still attempting to piece everything together.

"Laurie, what about her family?" I asked. "Did you meet them? Is she really close to them?" I didn't want to be too demanding. After all, the poor girl had been on an emotional roller-coaster for days. But there was so much I wanted to know.

"I met her parents, and they are wonderful people," Laurie answered with a smile. "Her mom and I started crying the minute we saw each other." Then her face clouded a little. "You know, Clare didn't have an easy life."

"What do you mean?" I asked, thinking that maybe there had been sickness, financial problems, or something similar.

"Her parents divorced when she was in first grade." Laurie's words paralyzed me. I couldn't speak as I processed this information. Bewilderment and anger rose in me. I thought, *God! We trusted You! We gave Clare to You and believed that you would take care of her!*

Laurie continued. "Both parents remarried and had families. Clare and her adopted sister spent the rest of their growing up years living for six months in one home, and then six months in the other."

I couldn't believe what I was hearing. We had trusted Clare's parents, too. They had promised to do everything in their power to give her the best home they could. Yet they had divorced and given her a broken family.

Then, that still small voice began to get so obnoxious I couldn't ignore it any longer.

"Yes," it told me, "they made mistakes. Haven't you? Didn't Laurie? Isn't this whole situation about a 'mistake'? How can you demand perfection from another human being? They did the best they could. They have loved Clare boundlessly and let her know that."

I took a deep breath, gave my inappropriate anger to the Lord, and acknowledged that He was more than able to keep His beloved child, our beloved child, through the emotional pain of a divorce.

Back in Portland, Clare e-mailed Laurie right away:

> Hi Hi!
>
> I tried calling you but I couldn't get the stupid phones to connect! Anyway, I was wondering if you were going to take the week and hang out or head on home. Your kids will be so happy and relieved to see you I'm very sure. Andrea especially, it sounds like! :)

Laurie did, indeed, feel pressure to get back home to her brood. It was an especially hectic time, as the family was moving into a new house. So, way too quickly, we had to put her on an airplane to South Carolina. It wasn't until after she had returned home that Laurie actually sat down and recorded the thoughts and feelings she had experienced the day she drove down to Portland to meet her daughter.

As I pressed the "play" button on the little recorder, I knew I wouldn't be disappointed.

> Hello Mama—
>
> I just realized that I never really filled you in about my trip to Portland to meet Clare.
>
> As I drove through Vancouver, I was thinking about the other times I had driven through there in my teens, and in the early years of our marriage. One time, during a weekend in Portland with my sisters, I stopped at a friend's house down there. She told me about a girl she knew who had been adopted and had just gotten married. She was a beautiful girl and married a good man, but she was going through a terrible time, dealing with severe depression and many rejection issues. Her words slammed

into my heart, and I knew that my daughter would no doubt go through a measure of that some time in her life, no matter what anyone said or did. That heaviness was hanging on me all weekend.

One night while we were there, my girlfriends and I dressed up and went out. On the way back to the house, I was driving alone for some reason. Halfway there, I thought about my daughter, who would be fourteen. I was hit with a sudden, deep, deep burden for her, weeping so hard I could barely see to drive. That was probably the most significant connection to her in all those twenty-five years, other than when I held her after she was born.

So here I was, driving into Portland again and having a feeling of connection and familiarity already. I got about two blocks from her house, and I pulled over. I didn't know what to do with myself. Didn't know whether to wet my pants or cry or jump up and down or what. So I just sat there for a few minutes. I was so nervous I had to force myself to drive on.

I pulled up in front of her house, a cool, old house, very quaint. I walked up those steep, cement steps and onto the porch, knowing that she could probably see me from the inside, but I couldn't see her. Thinking that she was on the other side of that big, wooden door. I walked across the porch, knocked on the door, and she opened it. And there she was, all tall and beautiful.

We just stood there looking at each other. Her boyfriend and another friend were sitting in the living room watching us. There were no tears. We were just standing in front of each other, staring at each other, then hugging on each other.

"I can't believe this is happening! And look at you!" I said.

We were both obviously nervous. She introduced me to her friends, and then we went upstairs, and she pulled out all the photo albums right away. It gave us something to lean on a little bit, being with each other for the first time. I was so numb and dazed, looking at all those pictures of a girl that I'd never known, but who looked so familiar, and all the pieces started coming together. I don't know how long we spent with the albums, probably a couple of hours. That night we had dinner together, and she put me in her bed. Then I was sleeping on her sheets and her pillows. Smelling her hair on the pillow.

The next night we went to meet Sue, Clare's mom, and her daughter, Clare's dad, Tom, his wife, Molly, and their daughters. They had made a special meal for us. We got acquainted over dinner and afterward they pulled out the baby pictures. Pictures of Clare with her parents. As I looked at them, I was struck by how much she looked like me, like Lynn's and Dawn's baby pictures, seeing the strong family resemblance. I was looking at her when I was hit with a huge wave of "Oh—oh—I don't know what to do with this."

There was one particular picture of Sue holding Clare in her lap, at maybe eight months or so. Sue looked so happy. But Clare looked nothing like her. I looked at this baby who was obviously a part of me. My baby. Thinking, *Who is that woman holding my baby? Why is she holding my baby?* Emotionally feeling *this isn't right!* but having to pass that by.

Clare and I went back to her house in different cars because we had picked up her car at the shop on the way to dinner. I got in my car, and Clare got in hers, and immediately I just lost it. I was getting on the freeway and driving down the road, with major tears pouring down my face. But more than tears, it was a groan from the depths of me over the agony of separation. I let myself feel the pain of my baby being with somebody else for all those years. And the pain of letting her go at birth was on me heavily. I let myself be there and grieve. I felt sick, almost to the point of throwing up, feeling the loss the way one does when there is a death. Feeling the intensity of the pain.

By the time I got to Clare's, I was pretty much wrecked, and I went to bed. In her bed. I listened to worship music for a while and then fell asleep. I know that this experience was a definite healing point for me. It was acknowledgment of a grief that you just kind of deal with while you are in it, when you are going through it. Some of it you bury, and your shields and mechanisms go up to keep you from feeling the depth of loss.

I am so thankful that I won't have to go to my grave with the enormity of that loss unrecognized. Not that God hadn't been doing a work in me through the years. He had. When Briana was born, something was completed in me. In my heart I was OK with the possibility of maybe never seeing Clare again. Though my highest desire was to meet her, I knew I could live without that if I had to. I knew that God knew what was best for me and what was best for her. So over the years I have had a deep knowledge that not meeting was OK and that God really was taking care of both of us.

The drive back to Seattle was awesome. We discovered how much alike we were emotionally, how we connected. Telling each other stories, stopping to get coffee, we talked the whole way. We were both so excited! We drove in the driveway and saw the banner that meant so much to Clare, and we both promptly started crying.

When I brought her to you I felt like I was bringing you a good gift. Over the years I've felt so many times that I let you down, that my life just brought—sadness. I don't mean that fully. I know that you love me, and I've given you good grandchildren and all that stuff. But Timothy and I went through so many ups and downs.

By this point I had received a great tear-bath. I just wanted to go and find Laurie and hold her, and tell her how much joy she has always brought to my life. That there is no real joy without pain. The bitter and the sweet.

But once again, there were three thousand miles between us. I left Clare a message on her cell phone, and soon received an e-mail from her:

> Hi, Granny!! Got your message late last night. . . . Thank you so much for calling. I was overjoyed. I'll be calling you back this afternoon when I get off work, so I hope you're around! It was amazing meeting you all. I almost have no words but sheesh! What an adventure this has been. I've found my tribe. :) That's how I feel about all this.
>
> I've felt alone for a lot of my life—not in a "world against Clare" kind of way, just that my parents were both involved in different marriages and families, and my younger sister and I spent our time shuffling back and forth between families feeling a little disconnected. That feeling has vanished from my soul. I belong, and I make sense and . . . I have a tribe! :) A very large one at that. . . .
>
> For the first time, I know where my heart is, and it's with you, my family. I just know I want to be there, and I want to be with you! So I will follow that, because it is a stronger need than anything I've had. I'll let the answers to all my many other questions be revealed as I go. Know that I love you and will call you later.
>
> xox   Clare

27
GLORY!!!

Indeed, Clare really meant business. Her job contract was soon coming to an end, and we all wanted her to move to Seattle so we could get better acquainted. As if all of this weren't enough excitement, we received the following e-mail from Laurie, addressed to Tom and me, Lynn, Carina, and Dawn:

> To the four fabulous females in my life and of course the Papa of all times,
>
> How incredible to get to share the events of reuniting with Clare and actually get to bring a healing gift to all of you to replace what initially brought much pain. I only wish Dawny could have been there, too. We shall have to have our own reunion.
>
> Since returning I have packed, cleaned, painted, said good-bye to a season and hello to a new one, recalled my story to many, moved into my wonderful home, and all of this now knowing for sure I am carrying my ninth child.

Wow! Crazy! Who would have thought having babies would truly become my full-time occupation?

Getting Clare back is the testimony of the power of love and God's heart to restore even when we choose a hard path for ourselves. She is the living, breathing word of life to this generation, which says there is a better way and that God has a desire for every living being.

Forgive my philosophizing. I am just so very moved and full of the goodness of God. I love you all and had such a special time there, so healing for me, for all of us.

I did not want to leave and could have used some rest, but it was a good thing that I came home. The family was running a little thin. Mama Andrea had had about enough, and Michael and Jadon nearly got in a fist fight the day I returned. That's the first time that's ever happened in their entire relationship!

So much more to say. I hope Clare does move to Seattle. Can't say I'm not a little jealous, but this isn't all about me now, is it? She needs you guys. I think life at the Carrs would be a little overwhelming for her. Then there is her birth dad and her need to also know him. It's hard to share. I do hope she can come be with us for a bit before she settles, though I haven't suggested that yet.

So, my dears, all is well though I miss you. We may be traveling to Seattle together. Just a thought at this time, so keep us in your prayers. It would be a good thing for all of us to be there. I love you. Also pray for my body to be strong and healthy through this pregnancy.

Your daughter, sister, friend—
Laurie

I didn't waste any time answering her e-mail:

> GLORY! I am in awe—speechless! How symbolic, full of promise and—GLORY! Well, what more is there to say? You said it all. So, my dear Laurie, may your womb be blessed once again. I guess it has been, my wonderful, amazing, strong, courageous, and fertile daughter! I'm so glad I didn't read this e-mail until this morning. I wouldn't have slept all night! Now I have all day to settle in. I am very proud of you and Timothy and your very blessed family. Yes, I will pray for health and strength, a supernatural portion of both.
>
> I have been thinking of you constantly because I know that the events with Clare had to be hard, though joyful. You got her back, but she is three thousand miles away, physically in our lives but not yours at the moment. How like the Lord to give you one more new life to nurture at the same time! And to think that you were actually pregnant when you met Clare!
>
> We are all excited at the prospect of having Clare nearby. As Carina was a "child" for you when Clare was born, so Clare is like a "sister" for Carina now. I've never seen Carina form such a quick, easy bond with anyone.
>
> So, my dear, you truly did bring us a healing gift that signifies the restoration happening in this family and in our church. Who knows how many more lives will be touched and healed along the way?! Give our love to everyone—with hugs all around till we can do it in person.
>
> Granny

The next e-mail we got from Clare said, in part,

Hi, My Loves!

Laurie's news!! It's amazing. I'm so, so, so excited to get to see my mom pregnant! I can't believe the blessings. Nine children! Whew! I just wish she was closer. I love you all and miss you like crazy. Give kisses to everyone for me. I'll be seeing you soon, soon, soon and living there before you know it.

xoxox   Clare

28
RICK-DAD

While she was in Portland with Clare, Laurie had given her daughter the contact information for Rick, her natural father. She told me, "Everything in me didn't really want to share her, but I knew it wouldn't be fair to keep the information from her. She needs to know her dad."

In the first part of July Laurie received an e-mail from Clare:

> Guess WHAT! I sent an e-mail to Rick—the basic "Hi, I'm Clare, I'm your daughter" introduction and this is what I got back just over an hour later. . . .
>
> Clare,
>
> > Well. It really is me, and I can't believe it's really you. I hope you didn't get my nose! I had named you Corinna, just so I could have a name for you. I have thought about you, wondered about you, written you letters on your birthdays, even kept a journal with you as my "muse" (which, I must say, was a thing

I completely dropped the ball on over the last several years. Sorry!).

Oh, man, my heart's beating like a rabbit. I don't even know where to begin. Suffice it to say that I'm out of my mind happy right now. I can hardly type, my hands are shaking!

I worried that perhaps you didn't want to find me. I heard so many different things about when it was legal or acceptable to begin the search. But I don't want to get into too much here on e-mail. There isn't a thing in the world that would make me happier than to see you.

I live in Seattle on Queen Anne (do you live in the NW?) and am leaving this Saturday on my annual motorcycle trip with my younger brother Dan. I have four brothers, I'm second to the youngest (47 next month . . . yikes!) My folks live in Bellevue in the same house where I grew up. I just want to keep typing, but would rather tell you this stuff in person. So, my daughter, when shall we meet?

I just re-read this e-mail and what a babbling mess it is! I'm sorry. I'm much more coherent in person!

. . . and just one day after Father's Day . . . good timing, Clare!

Rick

Clare here now. What a response, huh? Ha! More than I could have ever really expected. So this journey just continues! As I'm sure it will for quite some time. I am so blessed. It has got to be so rare for things to turn out this way. What an amazing plan He has for us. . . .

I love you! Talk soon, OK?

xo   C

Following is part of Laurie's answer to Clare:

—It is hard to be separated in body once again, but I know that there is One who knows exactly what you and I need. The specific events of the last weeks are no mistake. He is forming your heart, He is forming mine. Good stuff, the **bitter** and the **sweet** because it all makes for one big, sweeter gift as it plays out. Talk to you soon. I love you.

Your mom who had the privilege of carrying you in the womb,

Laurie

P.S. You were born for such a time as this.

Then July third, Laurie received this e-mail:

Laurie! My mom,

I miss you. Meeting Rick (wonderful; more in a bit) and having the two of you in my life and as a reference for myself, just knowing and loving you both has changed me beyond all reason. What wise words: "You were born for such a time as this" because it is so true! I feel completely realized, as I never have before. You are so right!

Do you remember that track on the Passion CD that was in Lynn's car on Sunday when were driving around? I found the artist and the song title. It's the David Crowder Band, "No One Like You." I can't stop listening to it. It makes me think of you.

So this weekend!! Rick came down to Portland. He was truly the last piece of the puzzle! Just amazing. The first sight of each other was much like you and me—laughing and shaking and hugging. He is so much more than I ever imagined he'd be. We spent the day walking around the city and looking at pictures and just enjoying each other, as you and I did! He had brought letters and his journal and TONS of pictures, including some of the two of you, which were great. That night after dinner, I went home and I crashed immediately. Yesterday we had breakfast together and spent the day running around old restoration shops (restoration?? again? amazing), climbing through piles of dusty old lamps and windows, vintage sconces and doors, and on and on. It was so surreal—the whole weekend. I couldn't have asked for it to be better, much like my weekend with you. Rick sent me an e-mail this morning and said this:

> "Please tell Laurie that I just simply said, 'Thank you!' It's the Biggest Thank You Known To Man, and I know I could be so much more verbose (!) and that will come, but for now, let her know I'm so happy and proud and completely blessed out of my mind. I know she'll understand. . . ."

So we'll have to talk more about this later but just know it was wonderful.

I've gotta try and work, impossible these days. Nothing matters to me like my family now. I just want to be near you.

Anyway I love you. Thank you for EVERYTHING. You amaze me every day and I don't stop thinking about you.

xoxoxoxoxox   Clare

Rick told Clare that when her fifth birthday came around, it had hit him especially hard that he had a real, live, five-year-old daughter—

somewhere. He wrote the following and sealed it in an envelope, hoping to give it to her someday. And that "someday" had arrived:

Happy fifth Birthday Little One—

I wish I could see you. This year, just as every other year since Laurie was married, I had a cake made with "Happy Birthday Corinna" on it, Corinna being the name I chose for you. Not knowing what your real name was, I felt the need to call you something other than "my daughter."

This must seem so strange for you to read, having a father all your life and then having someone you don't know calling you daughter. This is new for me, too, Corinna. Many times I've thought about writing you. Yet to write a letter to someone who may never get it is an odd thing. So I can only hope and pray that you will find me when the time comes. There isn't a day that goes by that I don't think of you, how you're growing, what you're learning. All I can say is, if the time comes, and you are reading this with your own eyes, then you have found me, and I am more happy than you can know.

The last few birthdays have been sort of small. Just me, your cake and candles, and a celebratory bottle of champagne. If this creates a lonely picture, I'm sorry. I'm having trouble finding someone to be with. Please don't misunderstand. There are a number of women to date, but I'm looking for a very special person. That takes time. Look at me. I'm writing my first real letter to you and I'm thinking about dating! What a schmuck!

There is so much to tell you I don't know where to start. If I start at the beginning, this letter will be a novel. Five inches thick! And besides, I'd really rather tell you about it in person (if that time comes). So I'll continue to tell you about my life now, and the past we can discuss another time.

Music is the most important thing in my life. It has some kind of connection to the innermost core of my soul and at given moments can move me to tears. I'm not talking about sad songs only. Fast songs—slow songs—happy songs—I think it's the pure emotion that an artist puts into a song that triggers this response with me. If the delivery is genuine, then the quality comes through, and I get goose bumps all over my body and this feeling in my chest like it's going to explode and my eyes fill up with water. It's great!

Anyway, it's because of this feeling that I decided to be a musician, if you can call drummers musicians. I wanted to be involved in a project that could do to others what it does to me. It makes me happy.

So it was because I was a musician that I met your mother, Laurie. It was the summer of 1981. My band played at her high school graduation party. I saw Laurie the minute she arrived. She was about seventeen, blond, tan, simply beautiful, and I went nuts! We met and ended up talking long after the party was over. So began this intense-but-sometimes-wacky relationship.

Her father was a minister, and they lived out in the country. I was raised Catholic but always felt like the church was too hypocritical. So, being young and kinda wild, I rebelled. I figured the only church I needed was myself, and I could pray just as well alone as I could in a crowded church. As long as I was a good person, I would be fine.

Well, I've learned a lot since then, and though I'm sure I haven't always been an angel, I try to be honest with everyone and keep things light and fun. Life is really too short to dwell on the negative. Just deal with it and move on.

The differences between Laurie and me, while a large part of the attraction, were also the reason for our demise. We dated through the summer until she left for Bible school in California. It was after she was there that she realized she was pregnant.

When she told me, all I could think was, "We can't get married. We're too young." But we were old enough to realize that marriages out of situations like this are seldom happy, and deep down, we were radically different. So that ruled marriage out.

This left three choices: have the baby and Laurie'd raise it herself, let a couple who is unable to have children but wants them adopt the baby, or have an abortion—out of the question. Laurie was too young to consider raising a child by herself; she knew that. I don't want you to underestimate the difficulty she had in making the decision, but ultimately, it was based on you and what would be best for you. So you would be raised comfortably by people who loved and needed you. So you'd be given all the love and opportunities that a new life deserves. The answer became obvious and the appropriate steps were taken to find the best home.

I'm sorry to say—truly sorry—that it was for music that in April 1982 I was unable to witness your birth in person. Apparently you were in a big hurry to make your appearance and showed up a week early. I was in a band, and on the last week of a three-week tour through Canada, Washington, Oregon, and California when I heard the news. I was in Pullman, Washington, playing at a college there, when I called home on Sunday the eighteenth to check in. My mom told me to call Laurie. I did, and she told me of your birth. I was so happy you were healthy and beautiful but so disappointed that I wasn't there.

All I have now is a picture of you at three months, and a letter from your new mother and father to Laurie, telling us some things about you. I'll show it to you when I see you. I can't tell you how much I think about that day when we meet. I'll be in my forties. Sounds old, but I'm sure age is only a state of mind.

I'm going to stop now, Corinna. But I promise more will come and you'll get them all and more someday. Anyway, have a wonderful and happy birthday, my love, and I'll write again soon. My dearest love to you every minute of every day,

Love,
Rick
There's so much to say.

29
MORE RELATIVES!

Y ou guys hurry back!" Sixteen-year-old Andrea Carr stood in the
driveway as Tom, Laurie, and I buckled up for the trip from
our home to Portland and Clare. We were driving the big, white van
that the Carr family (plus two extra passengers) had trekked all the
way from South Carolina to Washington in, arriving at our house a
couple of days earlier.

"Pray for us," I hollered out the window as Tom herded the large
vehicle down the drive. We had taken most of the seats out and were
on our way to move Clare out of her apartment and up to our house.
Soon we would be bringing her to the welcoming arms of the siblings
she had never met. The plan was for her to ride across the country in
the van and visit the Carrs for several weeks.

"I can't believe she is actually going back to South Carolina with
us!" Laurie's eyes betrayed awe and not a little uncertainty. "I wonder
how she will weather such a trip. I mean, it's one thing to meet all her
brothers and sisters, and another to hop in a van with all of us and
head across the country."

Tom chuckled. "From what we have seen of your Clare, I think she
will survive it all just fine." I agreed.

We drove down the shaded lane and stopped in front of the house Clare had been sharing with several roommates. As we climbed two short flights of concrete steps from the sidewalk to the porch, Laurie groaned a little but smiled, rubbing her now-bulging belly. Her cheeks were pink with anticipation and exertion. It had been four months since she had seen Clare.

She knocked, and when there was no answer, we went into the downstairs hallway. Laurie called Clare's name. We heard someone run from an upstairs room. Clare flew down the steps and into her mom's arms. Stepping back slightly, she poked at Laurie's tummy.

"Oh, look at you!" she exclaimed. Then poking again, and leaning down, so her new sibling could hear, she announced proudly, "Hey, I was the first one in there!"

Of course, all we wanted to do was sit and look at the two of them for the rest of the day. But time was limited and Clare had a doctor's appointment. She set about showing us where her belongings were so we could begin to load the van. Laurie went off in Clare's car to find some lunch for all of us, and after we had eaten hurriedly, Clare left for the doctor's office.

We made Laurie sit in a rocking chair on the porch while we wrestled boxes and furniture down the stairs, out the door, and then down the two last sets of steps to the van. Laurie fussed at her two aging parents and wanted to help, but we reminded her that any forty-three-year-old mother expecting her ninth child should probably be paying attention to her body when it complained.

When Clare returned, the three of us finished loading the van.

"Wow, look at that!" Clare's eyes were round with amazement as we slid the last chair into the spot Tom had been saving for it. "I never would have believed that it would all fit in there!" I was pretty amazed myself. My resourceful husband had packed it together like a jigsaw puzzle.

Tom and I hugged Laurie and Clare good-bye and drove back to Seattle. The two of them planned to sleep on a futon in the living room for one last night, so Clare could properly say good-bye to her friends.

The next day was Saturday, and in the afternoon the troops gathered. Lynn and Barry brought James, Rachel, and Mari over, and the rest of us waited impatiently for Clare's little red car to show itself. Timothy, Michael, Andrea, Jadon, Anna, Alyssa, and three-year-old Amber wandered around outside, enjoying another beautiful Seattle day. Matt, Carina, and their Nico, Tom, and I completed the welcoming committee.

Again we watched Clare leap out of the car and run toward her family, this time to her brothers and sisters and Timothy. I missed getting a picture when she hugged Michael, but I think I captured all the others on film. Big, teary grins, joyful hugs. No polite handshaking for this crowd. At one point, right after Clare had met her twin sisters, I snapped a picture of her holding both hands in front of her, smiling widely, and saying tearfully, "Look! My hands are shaking!"

Less than one week later, we were taking pictures again as Laurie and Timothy gathered their crew to head back to South Carolina. Clare completely blended into the scene as they stood beside the big, white van so we could record the occasion. There was already quite a load of belongings inside the van; and a loaded-to-capacity-and-then-some, white, single-axle trailer waited behind, ready to roll.

We stood in awe as all eleven of them piled in. We would definitely be praying as they rolled across the three thousand miles ahead of them. In fact we started right then, amidst tears.

A couple of days into the trip, we got a phone call from Laurie. She was laughing, a little hysterically, I thought. "Yes, we are parked along the freeway. The kids are sitting on the bank. One of the tires on the trailer blew out and damaged the fender. But everybody is OK!"

She started to say more, but someone needed her, and she hung up hurriedly. She called back a short time later to say, "All is well. Tire's fixed and we're back on the road."

A couple of days later the other trailer tire blew. Again, repairs were made and the trek continued. Nothing else too drastic occurred, and they arrived in South Carolina intact, though extremely road weary.

Clare spent a month with her family just getting acquainted. She finally got to meet her sister and brother-in-law, Briana and Gabriel, but had to leave just before their baby was born. Clare came back to us the end of October, intending to return to South Carolina in March for the birth of her new sibling, Laurie's ninth child.

30
FULL CIRCLE

A letter arrived from Laurie shortly after Clare returned from South Carolina:

Clare—

Thinking about you so much today. I'm actually taking a deep breath and moving into my third trimester, can't-stand-up-very-long, can-someone-do-my-grocery-shopping-for-me-please mode. My body is definitely transitioning to "slow down, granny. You do too much! Get ready to have this baby."

This forced slow down is teaching me new ways of walking in the Spirit instead of being depressed because I can't function normally, and cherishing the season because it is comparatively short.

I miss you. I miss at least having the opportunity to talk with you as things come up. I'm glad you are where you are. I know it's right and good for you. I can't help wishing we could give you what you need right here, but at the same time there is an ebb and flow to how this all works. I'm incredibly thankful that Gramps and Granny and all get to have you, and you them.

I looked at Timothy today and asked, "Do you ever get over the feeling that you want to or need to make up for all the lost years?" Yet there is something not quite right about that, and I really want to live in the fullness of today, not mourning the loss but celebrating what is current—the gift of love and time we share now.

I know it was pretty crazy and intense at times while you were here. You shared a bedroom with lots of girls (who love you like crazy by the way!), and you share my heart with many brothers and sisters. But there is only one Clare-shaped space in my heart, and I cherish that place daily. Always.

You are a gift to me and I thank you for so generously stretching to embrace all that my life entails. That takes a special person. I love you. Can't wait to share in our next season together and yet feel the richness of what is going on in both of us separately right now. God is good, so kind, so tender. Call when you can. I'll try again also.

Love you—

Me

After Clare was settled into her room at our home, she told us that Sue, her adoptive mother, wanted to come for a visit.

"Clare, you have more mothers and fathers and 'others' than anyone else I know!" I told her. "You are so rich in relatives!"

She laughed. "Yes, I've been thinking about my future wedding, which, by the way, only needs a groom, and counting how many close family members there will be. I think I lost count at one hundred and fifty!"

We were delighted when Sue came to visit. It was wonderful to meet the woman who had nurtured Clare and helped to form her into the amazing woman she had become. As she sat and talked with Tom and me, there was an immediate connection and bond.

"We are so thankful that Clare had you to love her," I said. "It's obvious from what she tells us and even from the pictures she's shared that you delighted in her."

"You've met her," Sue said. "You know that I was the fortunate one to have her all these years."

"But you're willing to share her with us," Tom said. "That's no small thing."

And it wasn't. I'd wondered if there would be feelings of competition or jealousy, perhaps carefully veiled; but there were none. Rather, there was friendship and appreciation, as she seemed to like us as much as we liked her.

She was a wise woman who realized that love is an elastic emotion that stretches to accommodate many in its embrace. She knew that the more people Clare had loving her, encouraging her, and praying for her, the better off she'd be.

That night in Clare's room, she and Sue giggled and cried together, praying for each other and talking into the night. Obviously, nothing had been lost in their relationship, only enhanced. Sue would always be "Mom" to Clare.

Then in November, we met Clare's dad. It was so good to see for ourselves the man who had written the beautiful piece that we found in the adoption agency's newsletter so many years before. The most obvious thing about this man was that he truly loved his daughter and wanted the best for her.

We knew there had to be a cost to both Sue and Tom for encouraging Clare to contact and reunite with her family of origin. I imagined it was something like giving one's daughter away in marriage, only harder. We had a good first visit with both parents and established the basis of ongoing friendships.

Meantime, across the country, as the weeks passed and Laurie's pregnancy progressed, her family members were increasingly alarmed at her size.

"Mom, you are huge!" was a common refrain. Having had one set of twins, she was a little nervous herself. But she also understood that having had eight children (including a cesarean delivery) could account for a super-stretchy body!

At one point, Clare had a very vivid dream about her mother's pregnancy. She dreamed that there were two babies, a big one, and behind it, a smaller one. When she told Laurie her dream, she found out that hers was not the first dream, but number six. All of the dreams, from various friends and relatives, were similar, and all were about two babies.

Laurie stayed amazingly even-tempered about it all, laughing at herself at every opportunity. The following e-mail came toward the end of January, from Laurie to Clare, Lynn, Carina, Dawn, and me:

> Hello, Girls!
>
> I wish just for a day we could all sit on my bed and laugh. Although when I laugh too hard, which Andrea causes me to do often, I feel like the baby/ babies? might slip out. That is, when I am standing up. When I am sitting, it just feels as though something might burst.
>
> Amber is in the tub with seven ponies. Alyssa is sitting at the foot of my bed singing, "It's-a-beautiful day for swingin' in the breeze—in the bre-ee-eeze in the trees. . . ." Jadon is doing schoolwork. Michael is popping ibuprofen. He just got his braces on today. Andrea is fluffing her hair so she can do her math. Anna is listening to tapes. I am supposed to be reading to the twins. Timothy is at work.
>
> Ah, peace, sweet peace. I love God. As I commandeer my life from my bed or the driver's seat of my car, I smile and drink chamomile tea, wondering how I will ever go back to running again. Peace and rest are great commodities in life, no matter what or who demands attention around you. Starts on the inside.

The second highlight of my week was dinner with my husband last night at McCormick and Schmick's, a gift from a friend and very elegantly pleasant. Mmmm, the scallops were good, good, good. As Eloise would say, "I just cawn't, cawn't, cawn't wait to go again."

The first highlight of my week . . . drumroll please . . . is love, plain and simple. Love being worked out in a crazy family. I get to wake up each day and love the wild man I married, work through personality crises with teenagers, and tame the passionate youngest three. Then I eat dinner with my married daughter (when her Gabriel is working) and my granddaughter! Very grand, might I add.

Amber is yelling, "Grandma! Can you get me out of the bathtub please?" Like I'm her grandma.

OK, successfully out and into her fairy suit. I hope she doesn't forget the wings. Maybe a halo would help.

Last, but certainly not least, my oldest child brings me great delight even though she is far away, but not really. Unspeakable even, the gift that you are.

OK, I'm getting teary.

On to the latest. Had a midwife check yesterday. I lost a pound, thank the Lord. It keeps me from tipping the scales to 180. Wow! I measured at 37 weeks, but actually I'm 34. There is only one evident heartbeat with a fetoscope. We decided that I probably just have one mysterious child in this belly. I came home thinking I'd better prepare everyone for one baby. The twinnies are really hoping for two babies. I'm actually glad to just set that aside.

Twenty minutes after I got home, I got a call from a friend named Ashley. She lives in Moravian Falls and is not up on all the dreams people have

had. Six people have had dreams about twins.
Ashley said, "I had a dream about you." I waited
to hear exactly what I thought I would hear. "We
were sitting together and I (Ashley) was holding
this tiny, preemie-size baby girl. Then you turned to
me holding another baby, and we switched. I took
the bigger, chunky baby, and you took the little
one. Then I sat up in bed and thought, *Those were
Laurie's twins!*"

What am I to think? Am I dense? Seven different dreams with the same element. Ashley knew
we were wondering about twins but not the other
stuff. If there is only one baby, what is the point of
the dreams?

So I will have an ultrasound Friday with the
other ultrasound tech. I want to see if she will do
some looking in other places.

Andrea has been entertaining me, singing,
"Cause I make you crazaayyy . . . just like youooo
. . ." which is now booming from Jadon's room.
Andrea's math is done. Her hair is fluffy. Her
complaint of "oh, my knees" brought her up off the
floor, and now we are "kung-fu fighting."

Time to move to the next phase of the day, find
out who's going out, who's making dinner. What
will Amber do? *Whoosh!* time for a nap.

> Love, love, love you all,
> Your daughter, sister, or mother
> Whichever category you feel I fit,
> Laurie

"I am so hoping that I can be there when that baby is born!" Clare
stuffed one last pair of socks into her suitcase, eyes shining with
anticipation. Departure was one day away and all seemed to be going
according to schedule. Now it was up to her new sibling(s) to make
sure that he/she/they didn't get in too big a hurry.

"Hey, Clare, let's go. We're going be late," Carina warned, hurrying into the room. "Besides, it looks like it might snow, so we'd better get a head start."

"Snow! It can't snow. My flight has to go out on time tomorrow!" Clare zipped her suitcase vigorously, emphasizing her words. She jumped up and pulled on her coat.

"Do you guys have to go out tonight?" I'd forgotten that they had a practice for their parts in an upcoming Good Friday service at church. They really needed to be there, because Clare would be in South Carolina all the next week.

At about 9:30 our phone rang.

"Granny! You have a new granddaughter!"

"Clare? What? Where are you?"

"We just left the church in a snowstorm, and I checked my messages. There was one from a friend of mine in South Carolina. She said, 'You have a new baby sister!' She said it happened really fast; no one knew what was going on. Nobody was in the room except Timothy and the midwife, but she's here! Her name's Kiley Joy."

She just couldn't wait, could she? I decided not to ask God any dumb questions, like "Why?" or "Where is the other baby?" and trust Him instead that everything was as it should be.

Clare's plane took off on time the next morning in spite of the weather. I sent an e-mail that would be waiting for her whenever she got around to looking at a computer:

> Clare—
>
> I'm thinking of you tonight with your mom and Timothy and your brothers and sisters, and praying that God will wrap you in His comfort. He loves you so much and will continue to take care of His little girl. I'll be praying for you all week, that you will know that He is with you, that you will know His embrace.
>
> It could feel a little fragmenting to belong to so many of us—but not when you understand how much we all love you and that you are every bit as

much a part of us as anyone who has grown up with this bunch!

I don't know what else to say to you except that I love you very much, and I know that God loves you even more, and He will prove it to you.

Have a wonderful week.

Granny

The e-mail Clare sent in return tells it all.

Today was divine.

And I don't mean that in a "Muffy and Buffy, this chocolate ganache is divine" kind of way.

I mean, today. was. divine.

It came on a soft and purposeful breeze through a window next to Laurie's bed and twisted my hair out from behind my left ear before settling in all four corners of that room. My baby sister's eyes kept scanning the ceiling above me as if she were watching the angels watch us as they protected, united, knit together our two hearts, an unexpected and glorious healing for a heart so long torn, it was blind to the break.

At first look, this day was fully lazy. I didn't leave my pajamas, didn't brush my teeth until 9:00 this evening, didn't even get my hair up off my neck until sitting down to write to you. I was in my Laurie's room for a straight ten hours, minus two trips downstairs for postpartum tea and a plate of food. (Yes, I ate dinner. Kind of.) Family and friends were in and out through the early afternoon, but come 3:30ish, I had mom and baby to myself.

The significance hadn't hit me until hearing Granny on speakerphone say, "Give your oldest daughter and your youngest daughter a kiss for me." The first and the last. The first, relinquished to

another family for twenty-four years, the last conceived the same month as our reunion. Significant?
I do think so. Upon Kiley's arrival, surprise! Not
the Joshua we were expecting, so I hadn't had the
mental prep to get my head around what it would
mean to me for this baby to be a tiny little girl.

Laurie had just finished feeding her as I sat back
down on the bed and mentioned, with tears on my
cheeks suddenly, that it's incredible to watch her
with Kiley because it's giving me the chance to see
how she would have been with me, how we would
have been together, had the Lord's plan allowed. My
imagination has gone there countless times since we
met in June, but this made it so real to me. . . .

I sat next to her and took little Kiley so Laurie
could get comfortable and sleep (sleep!). I need you
to picture this moment. If I'd had a vantage point
to take a photo I would have, but we'll just have to
wait until heaven to replay this. It will be worth the
wait. It was sweeter than words can describe.

I'm sitting on the bed, up against the wall,
on pillows, baby bundled in my arms, asleep and
beautiful and perfect in every way. She looks like I
did at a few days old. She has the birthmark on her
forehead and on the back of her neck, too. Laurie
is cuddled up, her head in my lap, sleeping and
breathing easily. It's sunny and cool outside, that
breeze still floating around the room, angels still
playing their music as only they can, little sisters
laughing and playing in the front yard. A moment
of peace.

I'm in awe and just staring at Kiley's tiny face.
In this moment this light enters my head, and I
know that the second little baby everyone dreamed
about is ME. And now I'm holding a newborn Elise
Joy, a newborn Clare Elizabeth. Holding the baby
that was me that day in April, 1982, who was given

into the Lord's hands for another mommy and daddy. And I'm crying, crying for what I lost when I was taken from Laurie, crying for what I found with my mom and dad, and crying for everything that has been returned. Crying and kissing Kiley/Clare's head and telling her that everything is going to be OK.

And then I realize that while I'm attempting to give something to this baby through my comforts and tears, she is giving back to me something I've not had these nearly twenty-five years. A baby me, nursed, cleaned, physically loved on by Laurie, was giving back to the grown-up me all those things I missed at the very beginning. Filling in cracks, mending hurts, curing rejection, healing old wounds.

We are connected, Kiley Joy and I, not only by name, but because of what she's done for me, what God has done through her for me. There's a golden thread sewn between our hearts, and as long as I live, I will never forget this afternoon, this divine exchange and the light she's given to me, simply by being. The Lord is so good and so faithful and makes *all things new.* There is nothing in this world that can keep His light shut out, His truth shut up, or His healing shut down. It breaks through all barriers even when we don't know how to see it and don't know how to ask for it. All we have to do is learn to receive it.

> He is Love, He is Love, He is Love.
> I love you guys more than
> I know how to say it . . .
> xoxox,
> Clare (both baby and adult version,
> new, all in one)

EPILOGUE

People tell us all the time how rich we are, and we often hear comments like "I wish I were a Lewis," or "Most people don't have what you have."

A growing sense of uneasiness began to creep into my heart as I heard this sentiment repeated time after time. I felt this disquiet because there is really nothing perfect about our family. We are all too human, with the failures and struggles that go with that humanity. I try to explain that in order to have restoration, something must have been broken. In some way, the original design must have been messed up.

My attempts to clarify are usually met with blank stares, or an "Oh, I know," when, really, they don't know. If they understood the night of pain we've lived through, they would never covet today's sunshine.

The whole *Bittersweet* story has grown out of failure and agony. There have been many years of waiting and wondering about "lost children." Individual lives and marriages have floundered at times, and there have been serious crises and skewed relationships.

Difficult things will always be there to resolve. The enemy of our souls will never give up in his attempt to bring death and destruction into our lives. He will constantly try to keep us from being the people that God created us to be. As long as we live on this earth, we will continue to make a mess of things.

But God has a very unusual exchange program: ". . . Beauty for ashes, the oil of joy for mourning, the garment of praise for the spirit of heaviness . . ." (Isaiah 61:3 KJV).

Clare has brought us much joy for mourning as has Shawn, but true restoration only happens when forgiveness is received from God, then granted to one another, and past hurts are healed. And none of these things can happen until we place all of the ashes, mourning, and heaviness in God's hands.

To each of you who share *Bittersweet* with us, may spiritual restoration be yours and may relational missteps find resolution.

                                                    —Gay Lewis aka Granny

APPENDIX

Abortion Methods

This information was excerpted with permission from *When You Were Formed in Secret / Abortion in America*, by Gary Bergel with essay by C. Everett Koop, Intercessors for America, © 1980–1998, www.ifapray.org.

D & C or dilatation and curettage abortion: This method is most often used in the first thirteen weeks of pregnancy. A tiny, hoe-like instrument, the curette, is inserted into the womb through the dilated cervix, its natural gateway. The abortionist then scrapes the wall of the uterus, cutting the baby's body to pieces. It is now used less frequently than suction.

Suction abortion: Most commonly used method for early pregnancies, the principle is the same as in the D & C. In this technique . . . a powerful suction tube is inserted through the cervix into the womb. The body of the developing baby and placenta are torn into pieces and sucked into a jar.

Salt poisoning, or Hyper-Natremic abortion: This method is generally used after the first thirteen weeks of pregnancy. A long needle is inserted through the mother's abdomen, and a strong salt solution is injected directly into the amniotic fluid that surrounds the child. The salt is swallowed and "breathed" and slowly poisons the baby, burning its skin as well. The mother goes into labor about a day later and expels a dead, grotesque, shriveled baby. Some babies have survived the "salting out" and have been born alive.

Hysterotomy or cesarean section abortion: Used in the last trimester of pregnancy, the womb is entered by surgery through the wall of the abdomen. The tiny baby is removed and allowed to die by neglect or sometimes killed by a direct act.

Prostaglandin chemical abortion: This is the newest form of abortion and uses chemicals. These hormone-like compounds are injected or otherwise applied to the muscle of the uterus, causing it to contract intensely, thereby pushing out the developing baby. Babies have been decapitated during these abnormal contractions. Many have been born alive. The side effects to the mother are many. A number of mothers have even died from cardiac arrest when the prostaglandin compounds were injected.

Today (2008): All of the above methods are still being used as described, though there is more caution about using the Prostaglandin method because of dangers encountered. The newest methods are in pill form. All of these pills can be readily researched on the Internet, but one must spend some time to make sure one is getting the whole story.

The morning-after pill: These pills (ECPs), if taken before ovulation, can act as a contraceptive. However, if taken after fertilization has occurred, they can cause an abortion by preventing the embryo from implanting in the womb. Besides causing the aftereffects of nausea, vomiting, dizziness, etc., it has been found that women who use this drug have an increased risk of tubal pregnancy. This type of

pregnancy, which occurs in the fallopian tubes, can be very danger-
ous or even fatal if not discovered early enough.

The abortion pill, Mifepristone (RU-486 or Mifeprex): This is an
artificial steroid that deprives the baby of nutrients and stops its
development and causes death. Often a second drug is given later
(Misoprostol) to cause contractions and expel the detached baby
from the womb.

Methotrexate: Another drug used to terminate pregnancy.

We would love to hear from you!
Do you have restoration stories to share?
Questions for any of us?
Send a confidential message to one of us at:
info@bittersweetthebook.com
You can also e-mail us to find out about our speaking, musical,
and media events;
or go to www.bittersweetthebook.com

See pictures, leave us a message, read news at
www.myspace.com/bittersweetthebook